THE HISTORY
OF THE
135th SIEGE BATTERY

Major C. P. Heath, D.S.O.
In command of the Battery from January, 1917, until its disbandment in August, 1919.

THE HISTORY

OF THE

135TH SIEGE BATTERY

R.G.A.

COMPILED BY

LIEUTENANT D. J. WALTERS, M.C., R.G.A.

AND

AND LIEUTENANT C. R. HURLE HOBBS, R.G.A.

with a Foreword by

BT. LIEUT.-COLONEL C. S. S. CURTEIS, C.M.G., D.S.O.

The Naval & Military Press Ltd

published in association with

FIREPOWER
The Royal Artillery Museum
Woolwich

Published by
The Naval & Military Press Ltd
Unit 10 Ridgewood Industrial Park,
Uckfield, East Sussex,
TN22 5QE England
Tel: +44 (0) 1825 749494
Fax: +44 (0) 1825 765701
www.naval-military-press.com

in association with

FIREPOWER
The Royal Artillery Museum, Woolwich
www.firepower.org.uk

In reprinting in facsimile from the original, any imperfections are inevitably reproduced and the quality may fall short of modern type and cartographic standards.

The Crucifix at Roclincourt.

DEDICATED

TO

THE MEMORY OF THOSE GALLANT SOLDIERS

WHO GAVE THEIR LIVES WHILE
SERVING WITH THE BATTERY,
1916 — 1918

"Thy days are done, thy fame begun;
Thy country's strains record
The triumphs of her chosen Son,
The slaughters of his sword!
The deeds he did, the fields he won,
The freedom he restored!

"Though thou art fall'n, while we are free
Thou shalt not taste of death!
The generous blood that flow'd from thee
Disdain'd to sink beneath:
Within our veins its currents be,
Thy spirit on our breath!

"Thy name our charging hosts along
Shall be the battle-word!
Thy fall, the theme of choral song
From virgin voices pour'd!
To weep would do thy glory wrong—
Thou shalt not be deplored."

Byron.

FOREWORD

BY

BT. LIEUT.-COLONEL C. S. S. CURTEIS, C.M.G., D.S.O.

The Battery whose history follows formed part of the 83rd Brigade, R.G.A., from December, 1917, to December, 1918.

During that critical and eventful year they were fortunate in keeping their commanding officer, Major C. P. Heath, D.S.O., throughout.

Of the Battery and its commanding officer it is difficult to speak too highly. To say that they never failed to do their duty, and that I cannot recall a single instance of their allowing circumstances to defeat them, will probably convey more to soldiers than praise in any less measured terms. A battery of 8-inch howitzers on Vickers platforms is a most difficult equipment to get satisfactory results from. Being on wheels, something is expected of it in the way of mobility. Yet the platform is practically as cumbersome and difficult to lay as that of heavier natures. Again, the design was from the first faulty, so that no matter how perfect the laying of the platform, difficulties, far from ending when once in action, rather increased. It was a compromise between a gun of position and a mobile gun, and was full of inherent weaknesses, particularly of the rear baulk, and was probably the most difficult equipment in the service to keep in action and obtain the full rate of fire from. With the never-ending and heavy labour that such an equipment involves I can say that no battery of a similar nature ever overcame its difficulties more successfully or with less trouble to others.

The winter of 1917-18 found the Brigade on the Vimy Ridge—the Arleux-Oppy-Gavrelle front, in the XIIIth Corps—and in immediate support, first of the 47th Division, and afterwards of the 56th Division. The Brigadier-General commanding Heavy Artillery was Brigadier-General L. W. P. East, C.M.G., D.S.O.

To get at enemy batteries it was necessary to keep about half the Brigade well forward of the Ridge around and in front of Bailleul Village. The Battery had one section in Bailleul. But for a certain amount of cover from ruined buildings and artificial screens, every flash was in full view of the enemy. That winter saw the first use of "mustard gas" shell in any quantity by the enemy; and the proximity and visibility of the guns to the enemy, combined with the fact that preventive measures against the new gas were not perfected in a day, caused considerable casualties at the forward guns. The forward section was frequently relieved and the whole Battery shared the trials and dangers of anything but an easy winter. They did much good counter-battery work and the fire of the enemy was well kept down.

Some time before the great German offensive of 1918, the 56th Division relieved the 47th Division, and when, about March 23rd, it became plain that an attack on the Ridge and Arras was imminent, practically all artillery was withdrawn to behind the Ridge. Two sections R.F.A. only were left. This withdrawal made it impossible for the R.F.A. to do more than just cover our front line.

On the evening of March 27th, and with perfect observation from the Ridge, the enemy were twice, at about 4 and 5.30 p.m., seen massing in the Fresnes-Rouvroy line. The accurate fire of the Battery and the remainder of the Brigade distributed along this line of trenches (the R.F.A. were, unfortunately, out of range), in two heavy and sustained bursts of fire of about half an hour each, bolted the enemy across the open in large numbers, and did something towards taking the steam out of the attack on the following morning.

The part played by the Battery on the following day, under prolonged and heavy fire by several enemy batteries with H.E., gas, and shrapnel, was worthy of its reputation; and men of the Battery can always remember with pride that they played their part in what was a heavy and costly defeat of the enemy in his attempt to take by assault the southern end of the Vimy Ridge, the great buttress that was probably the key to our whole front from Amiens to Ypres.

It is sufficient to say that at 5.30 p.m. on March 28th, his final attack on Bailleul East Post was completely defeated, and he never afterwards made a further attempt against the Ridge. The 56th Division, though compelled during the battle to withdraw to prepared positions at the foot of the Ridge, fought a great fight and, originally weak in numbers, suffered heavy casualties. The losses inflicted on the enemy by machine-gun fire and a mixed barrage of field and heavy artillery were enormous.

The Division was relieved by the 4th Canadian Division, and the Canadians in their turn by the 51st Highland Division.

Nothing eventful occurred on this front from April to the end of July, when the Battery proceeded, with the rest of the Brigade, to the Amiens Sector to take part in the final advance.

From August 8th to November 11th, 1918, the Brigade was with the Fourth Army—the Canadian Corps, the XXXIst French Corps, and the XIth Corps, and in immediate support of the 3rd Canadian Division, the French 47th and 126th Divisions, the 1st Division, 6th Division, 32nd Division, and the 46th Division.

In the more rapid movement of the advance the Battery could not be employed, but for some time they did excellent work with captured 15-cm. howitzers and 10-cm. long-range guns. Whenever the least check occurred, notably before Parvillers, Ham, the Hindenburg Line at Bellenglise, and other places, the Battery was quickly in action and doing invaluable work.

In a particularly nasty position in Holnon Wood, near Attilly, some 3,000 yards from our front line, the Battery and Brigade were subject to continuous shelling and several very heavy concentrations of fire, which caused many casualties to guns and men. In spite of this the Battery did its work, and moved, after ten days or so, to take part in the great bombardment preceding the wonderfully successful assault of the Hindenburg Line at Bellenglise by the 46th Division. In this bombardment the Battery achieved a fine performance as regards sustained rate of fire, and followed it by a remarkably quick night move.

After the Armistice I said good-bye to the Battery at Wassigny, where they were billeted in December 1918, and may mention that it was the only Battery of my Brigade that I was able to see and say good-bye to as a Battery.

The others dribbled away man by man until reduced to cadre strength.

I am glad of this opportunity of again telling them what an honour it was to command such batteries and such men in such great fighting, and what a pride I took in them and their deeds. Every officer and man may well feel great pride in having served in such a fine fighting battery.

I am sure they will look back, as I do, on the fighting we were able to do together in the Great War as the greatest work of their lives, and I sincerely hope that none of them have reason to regret the brave and loyal service they gave to their country in its hour of need.

C. S. S. CURTEIS,

Bt. Lieut.-Colonel.

COLOGNE,

January, 1921.

The Battery in Action near Henin, May, 1917.

PREFACE

In compiling the pages which follow, we have not addressed ourselves to the task of preparing a new War Book for the consumption of the reading public generally, neither do we presume to have produced a work possessing either artistic or literary merit. All that is claimed for the present volume is that it provides an accurate record of a Battery which, during its service in France, pursued with the utmost vigour the task of beating the enemy. As a plain record of facts it is feared that, to the general reader, the text may prove tedious and, in places, unintelligible. The book, however, is intended primarily for those who, as members of the Battery, constitute, so to speak, the *dramatis personæ*, and it is hoped that its pages may help to keep fresh in their memory the outstanding incidents of those strenuous years when, as comrades in arms, we all pulled together for victory.

In various parts of the text some mention has been made of good work done by individual members of the Battery. We feel, however, that many acts of personal valour, which were performed so unobtrusively as to attract little notice, have unconsciously been omitted. To those responsible for such deeds we desire to make this acknowledgment and to ask to be absolved of any wilful intention of excluding mention of them.

Our grateful thanks are due to Bt. Lieut.-Colonel C. S. S. Curteis, C.M.G., D.S.O., for so kindly undertaking to write the foreword; to those who, by contributions or suggestions, have helped to make our task the easier, and to all who have promised to give the book their support when it leaves the hands of the publishers. Major C. P. Heath, D.S.O., our greatly esteemed O.C., is responsible for the sketch maps where they occur, and we would add that it is doubtful whether the book could have been written but for the valuable material supplied by him and the no less valuable encouragement which we have derived from the keenness and enthusiasm which he has displayed throughout the preparation of the work. The plan and section of the B.C. post at Nieuport have been kindly contributed by Lieutenant W. D. Hooper, R.G.A., and for the photographs of the church and pits at Bailleul, we are much indebted to Lieutenant E. J. Noakes, R.G.A.

In conclusion, we shall be glad to have brought to our notice any errors of fact which may have crept into the text, or any omissions or inaccuracies in the appendices. The records from which the latter have been compiled are not, by any means, complete, and it is possible that some names have been left out which should have been included.

D. J. W.

C. R. H. H.

January, 1921.

CONTENTS

APPENDICES

ILLUSTRATIONS AND MAPS

DIAGRAMS AND MAPS,

By Major C. P. Heath, D.S.O.

DRAWINGS,

By Lieut. W. D. Hooper, R.G.A.

WATER COLOUR DRAWINGS,

By Lieut. C. R. H. Hobbs, R.G.A.

PHOTOGRAPHS

ILLUSTRATIONS AND MAPS

PHOTOGRAPHS

facing page

ORDNANCE MAP

Note.—The location of places mentioned in the text are referenced to the squared maps used in France.

One of the Battery's Mark V Howitzers in Action near Henin, May, 1917.

CHAPTER I

THE FORMATION OF THE BATTERY

[MAY, 1916]

In the first stages of the Great War the British Army in Flanders was fighting under a severe handicap, in that the Artillery in all its branches was not adequate enough to render it any real support or protection; and it was obviously essential that we should create, as rapidly as possible, a very large and powerful force of Artillery of all kinds if we were to have any prospect of victory.

For many reasons this force could be brought into being only very gradually; but at the end of 1915 the production of guns, ammunition and other equipment was proceeding at such a pace and the facilities for training officers and men had been so developed that the War Office were able to get really started on this task. All through the spring of 1916, Batteries were being formed and trained with amazing rapidity; and such progress was made that it was possible to send out many of these Batteries in time for the Somme offensive in July, 1916. There we had over one hundred Siege Batteries of varying calibres from 15-inch to 6-inch—a great improvement on the state of affairs in September, 1914, when we had only six Siege Batteries, formed from the three Siege Companies in England at the outbreak of war.

It was during this period that the 135th Siege Battery came into being. A W.O. letter dated 3rd May, 1916, had given birth to this Battery; it was to be formed at Tynemouth under the parental care of the C.R.A. Tynemouth Garrison.

Within a few days Battery Sergeant-Major Lovett and a Quarter-Master-Sergeant reported at Tynemouth, and early on the morning of Monday, May 22nd, Lieutenants D. J. Walters and S. R. Wood arrived from the school at Lydd after a night's journey from London. They reported to the C.R.A., who was most anxious that they should set to work at once to collect the men and get the Battery really into life without any further delay.

Accordingly Lieutenant Wood went off at once to Cullercoats—a small seaside town a mile or so north of Tynemouth—in search of accommodation for the officers and men; while Lieutenant Walters interviewed the C.O.'s of the 47th and 12th Co.'s R.G.A., which were stationed at Tynemouth, and from which the gunners were to be drawn. An inspection of each company was arranged and the most promising men were selected for the new Battery. Later in the day Lieutenant Wood returned and reported that he had taken over a rather dilapidated Temperance Hotel in Cullercoats to accommodate the men, and near this was a field which we should be allowed to use as a parade ground. Billets for the officers were found on the sea front and within a hundred yards or so of the men's quarters. That night the Battery—consisting of two officers, a B.S.M., a Q.M.S. and a corresponding number of valises and kit bags—moved into Cullercoats.

Next day ten N.C.O.'s arrived from B Depot (Bexhill) together with a party of signallers—three N.C.O.'s and eight men from the A Depot (Bexhill); and on Wednesday morning we took over the gunners selected from the Tynemouth Companies—sixty-six from the 12th Company and forty-four from the 47th Company. They were a splendid lot of fellows. Nearly all of them were Derby recruits with only a few weeks' experience of the Army; but they were very keen to learn their job and most anxious to do the right thing, and consequently everything went well from the very beginning. The N.C.O.'s, too, looked a sound lot—one or two had already seen service in France; and altogether we had the material to make a very good Battery.

Early next day it was distinctly alarming to hear that we had to present ourselves at the Fort (Tynemouth) in the afternoon to be inspected by the G.O.C. Siege Artillery—General Nichols. Fortunately we had no rifles, so the morning was spent in a feverish effort to learn the elements of foot drill; and after dinner the Battery marched down to the Fort in the charge of two very anxious officers. However, the inspection was a great success; the men were splendid and the General expressed himself as being "highly satisfied with their quality and smartness."

We were none too comfortable in our "hotel" which was very draughty and leaked badly. The humorists wasted no time, and the rooms were soon placarded with such notices as: "This way to the shower baths," "Bright and Breezy Villa," etc. Before the end of the week everybody had become thoroughly accustomed to his new surroundings and the men had been quick to make new friends.

We attended our first church parade on the Sunday (May 28th). On the way we met the C.R.A. with Captain D. B. C. Sladen, who had come to take command. Lieutenant Walters returned with him to Cullercoats, leaving Lieutenant Wood—much to his annoyance—to perform the delicate operation of conducting the Battery through its first church parade. On the following day Lieutenants C. E. Lucas Phillips and E. G. Richardson were posted to us from Horsham.

Captain Sladen soon got to work. The Battery was organised into sections and sub-sections; and the greater part of the time was given up to foot drill and physical training, with occasional route marches. Also classes were begun for layers, observers, B.C.A.'s and signallers; and when the Battery was ordered, a few days later, to move to Horsham, every one had been fitted more or less into his place and had learnt a little about his job as an artilleryman. In less than a fortnight we had grown into a real live unit, proud of our name and imbued with a keen determination to acquit ourselves well in all the trials which were before us.

The Garrison Band escorted us to the station, where a number of friends had assembled to give us a very hearty send-off. We left Tynemouth late on the evening of Saturday, June 4th, and after travelling all night arrived at Horsham, in Sussex, about six o'clock next morning.

CHAPTER II

The Battery in Training

[June—August, 1916]

The camp was a mile or so out of Horsham—a delightfully pretty place. It consisted of a number of large tin huts which furnished a very comfortable home for our men. Many batteries were in training here, all about the same "age," and all were grouped together as one Brigade —R Brigade.

The camp had its staff of instructors, and a certain number of guns were available for drill purposes. The gunners learnt something of their gun drill; dug-outs were constructed and each detachment learnt to lay a gun platform. There was also equipment for the "Specialists," dial sights for the layers, directors for the B.C.A.'s, and some flags and telephones for the signallers.

We spent a strenuous month here, and on July 4th we moved to Lydd, on the south coast of Kent, to complete our training. *En route* we were joined by Lieutenant K. F. Allen (Hants R.G.A.), who completed our establishment of officers. On arrival we were attached to B Brigade, to be transferred a few days later to C Brigade. The men were billeted in Brick Town—the most comfortable quarters in the camp—and the officers in the R.A. Mess.

Life was now one endless rush; we had physical drill before breakfast and gun drill for the rest of the day, except for occasional practice in platform laying and dug-out construction in the sand and shingle. After a fortnight we were considered to be sufficiently advanced to begin our firing practice. This was always a most trying ordeal for the officers—and the C.O. in particular—as all "shoots" (especially the best!) were ruthlessly dissected and criticised by the School Commandant and his staff of instructors in the presence of all the officers of the camp. These shoots we carried out with fair success, although there were a number of "incidents."

Our final shoot will live long in our memories. It attracted all the Camp Staff, most of them going down to the observation post, leaving one or two to look on in the battery position ; while some of their underlings dashed up and down the range on horseback carrying red flags (a very necessary precaution, as it happened). From the outset they criticised everything, and the unfortunate officer at the O.P., whose duty it was to control the shooting, was soon in a state of hopeless panic. Orders were reeled off by phone to the Battery, only to be cancelled immediately ; and this went on for some time until most of us were in just as bad a state of "nerves" as he. At last we got off our first round. There was an ominous pause—then frantic buzzing on the phone, followed by a long and animated conversation between one of the officers at the guns and the School Commandant at the O.P. It appeared that the first round had missed the O.P. by only a few yards, and after a long inquiry it was discovered that the much-harassed O.P. officer had been so confused by the interference of the Staff that he had muddled all his calculations and laid the gun on the O.P. !

Before the end of July our training period was over and about half the Battery were sent off on mobilisation leave—their last leave. On July 29th the remainder entrained for Bristol to mobilise, a small party under Lieutenant Wood proceeding via Woolwich to pick up gun stores and other equipment.

By this time we had saved a considerable amount of money on the Battery's messing account, and with this a field cooking range, some boxing gloves, a gramophone and various games were bought for use on active service. Every one will agree that the cooking range was a splendid investment and one of our best friends throughout our sojourn in France.

At Bristol we were quartered in what was called the White City, which turned out to be an extremely dirty and dilapidated collection of wooden sheds. Originally it had been an exhibition, modelled on the White City at Shepherd's Bush, and there were still traces of its former splendour and glory. The Elizabethan village was still there and parts of it were used for the officers' mess. Some of the men slept in what had once been the jungle—a huge shed whose walls were covered with coloured paintings and a few carvings of fierce and wild beasts. Rumour said that the ghosts of its former occupants still lurked in this jungle in the form of animals, which though they made no pretence to greatness in stature, yet fell only a little short of their forerunners in their man-biting capabilities.

On the Sunday a printed letter came from the railway company which stated that some goods for us had been waiting so long at the sidings that demurrage charges would have to be paid unless we removed them at once. On inquiry it transpired that the aforesaid "goods" consisted of four 8-inch howitzers (each weighing about fourteen tons) and one or two other small items.

Accordingly an officer and a party of men set out immediately for the station, and having succeeded in borrowing a rather worn-out and overworked caterpillar, we spent the rest of the day in hauling these guns up to the camp. Our route lay across the City, and, what with the noise of the caterpillar and the size of the guns, we created no small stir. On our rather laborious journey to the camp we gradually collected all the urchins, perambulators and dogs of the neighbourhood. These children and dogs swarmed all over and under the guns whenever we halted, and it was quite a comic procession which escorted us into the camp.

We spent a happy time at Bristol. Our hard work was over and there was nothing to do except to check the stores as they arrived and to learn something about them. The Bristol people were very kind and friendly—especially the girls—and most of us had our time fully occupied in the evenings!

There were many promotions to bring the number of N.C.O.'s up to establishment, while a few veterans who were found to be unfit at the last moment had to give place to new men—much to everybody's regret. Our artificers, too, had been sent to us: Staff-Sergeant Band, who joined at Lydd, and Wheeler Corporal Nicholson and Fitter Hill, who came to us at Bristol.

There were many false alarums before we received our embarkation orders. The Battery was preceded by an advance party which left on August 11th; consisting of Captain (then Lieutenant) Phillips, Sergeant Jack, Corporal Unsworth, Corporal Lockley, "Busty" Jackson and a dozen others. They had an eventful journey to France, and finally, after having afforded much diversion for R.T.O.'s, they found themselves at the IIIrd Corps H.A. Rest Camp (Fourth Army) in the little village of La Houssoye, a few miles behind Albert.

On the 13th the guns and the A.S.C. column—composed of four caterpillars, over thirty Commer lorries, a Daimler car and four or five motor cycles and side-cars—which had joined us a few days previously, were taken to Avonmouth, whence they were shipped to France. Finally, the Battery itself entrained at Bristol at midnight on August 18th and received a very hearty send-off from the large crowd of friends we had made there. Proceeding via Paddington and Victoria we reached Folkestone at 8 a.m. on the 19th. We rested at Shorncliffe Camp until the afternoon, when we marched down to Folkestone Harbour, and at 3.15 embarked on the *Golden Eagle*. Soon all was ready, and at 3.50 we slowly set out on our journey across the Channel under the care of a destroyer. We landed at Boulogne at 5.40, and straightway marched to St. Martin's Camp, some two miles out of the town.

We were all very tired, and after we had obtained some food we turned in to our tents for our first night's sleep in France. It had been a memorable day in our lives. We were sad yet happy, too—happy to feel that at last our turn had come to take our place in the fighting line.

CHAPTER III

The Somme Battle

[August--November, 1916]

We remained at Boulogne for two days while the guns and transport were being unloaded from the ship, and on the evening of August 21st we set off, equipped with an interpreter, by train for an unknown destination, leaving the guns and transport to come on by road.

Early on the 22nd we detrained at Longeau Station (near Amiens), whence we were taken in lorries to join the advance party at La Houssoye. They, we found, were none too happy. Before leaving England they had been told that they would be required to prepare a battery position. Nothing of the sort happened. They were kept hanging about for ten days with nothing to do; and, having been forbidden to take any kit with them, they shivered for the first two nights without blankets. Eventually they managed to borrow (or at least they said they borrowed them !) one blanket per man from the sympathetic Siege Park. Captain Phillips looked none too well—he had lost his safety razor on the way up and had cut his face into a wonderful pattern in his praiseworthy efforts to shave with a second-hand service razor !

The day after arriving at La Houssoye we received the unwelcome order to split up : the Right-Half Battery, with Major Sladen, Lieutenant Allen and Second Lieutenant Walters, were to be attached to 57 Siege Battery ; and the Left-Half, with Captain Phillips and Second Lieutenants Wood and Richardson, to 19 Siege Battery. The object of this was to initiate us gradually in the gentle art of war under the guidance of tried and hardy veterans.

After dividing up the Battery stores and saying good-bye to our interpreter, the Right-Half Battery started up the line on August 25th, the Left-Half following on the 28th. What our feelings were it is difficult to say. They were certainly very mixed; we were glad we were going into *the* battle area, the famous Somme, about which all the world had been talking for six weeks; but we did not at all like being split up, and we were inclined to regard it as a blot on our escutcheon that we should be considered incapable of going straight into action "on our own." However, looking back on it in the light of experience, one is inclined to think that the authorities were wise, after all.

The Left-Half Battery went into action alongside 19 Siege Battery just outside the village of Mametz on the Mametz-Carnoy road. Major A. H. Moberly, D.S.O., was in command of 19, and we soon fitted in pretty well with that famous Battery. The Right-Half Battery was split up still further; No. 1 gun going to the forward section of 57 Siege Battery near Contalmaison, and No. 2 to their rear section at Fricourt.

Thus did "135" get its first taste of war. These battery positions were not worried much by shells and the conditions were not too bad. However, in this period the gunners gained valuable experience on the guns, and the officers and signallers went up the line for their first taste of forward observation work, and some of them received their "baptism of fire" under very trying conditions at High Wood and Delville Wood.

We remained with 19 and 57 S.B.'s for upwards of a month, when the Battery re-united behind the line at Viviers Mill on September 21st. That same evening we were split up again, to our intense disgust, and sent to two other batteries. The Right-Half went to 67 Siege and the Left-Half to 47 Siege, both close to Montauban, and in the XVth Corps Heavy Artillery (Brigadier-General P. Hamilton).

The Battery had a new experience this time—that of moving forward to new positions; this, perhaps, is the hardest job the heavy gunner has to do. From these positions we took part in the famous attacks of September, when our infantry drove the Hun from Delville and High Woods and the villages of Flers, Guillemont and Guinchy; and later pushing on a little farther captured Gueudecourt in the first Tank attack.

At last the Battery was to be finally reunited. We were placed under 14th Heavy Artillery Group (Lieutenant-Colonel Collingwood), and ordered to advance from our positions behind the Montauban ridge, to four emplacements on the Longueval-High Wood road.*

The men had been working pretty hard for a fortnight, but now they were in for a nigger-driving, back-breaking time. On the morning of September 29th a party was sent out to begin work on the new position and to lay platforms; the left section pulled in on the night of September 30th—October 1st, and the right section followed next night.

If we had gained some experience working with our guardian batteries, we certainly gained far more when we pulled in on our own, for the first time we had to keep hard at it all night and far into the next day. The piece of road into the position was bad and treacherous and the gun crews were already weary after their day's work. Still they laboured on in the mud and rain, wet to the skin, all through the night, till at last in the early morning the guns were safely on their platforms.

The following days were just as strenuous, for there were dug-outs to build and ammunition to get down to the position. Not one of those who were at Longueval will ever forget that ammunition job. Lorries could not come nearer than 500 yards of the position, i.e., to the cross-roads on the Longueval-Bazentin road, where they unloaded in a great hurry and dumped the shells anywhere in the mud. The wretched gunners had to dig these out and carry them to the guns, and this at a time when we were firing about 300 rounds a day. That is, roughly, thirty tons of ammunition had to be carried down to the guns each day by the gun crews whose misfortune it was to be off duty. The whole place was a sea of mud: it rained incessantly and the men got soaked to the skin; and they slept in their clothes to dry them, only to get wet through again next day. We resorted to all possible means of transportation: some shells were dragged along by ropes, others laboriously pulled down by "trench carts" or improvised sledges. Later the Major got the Engineers to lay a Decauville; but the gradient was so steep that it was no easy matter to prevent the heavily laden trucks from slipping off the muddy rails and upsetting their cargo into the mud alongside. Later still we were provided with fatigue parties from the British West India Regiment—the "Christy

---

* About S. 11c. 1.4. Sheet 57 c S.W.

Minstrels," as one of our wags aptly described them—which gave our men a certain amount of respite. Still there is no doubt about it that these were appallingly hard times for a Battery occupying its first position. For a long time after "the cross-roads" was a by-word. It stood for all that was thankless, disheartening and back-breaking, and conjured up a picture of the most trying period in the whole history of the unit—not excluding those "shell humping" days at Gentelles Wood in August, 1918.

We made "billets" on the reverse slope of the hill behind us—in the old German line. There we were afforded constant diversion by the dug-outs falling in on us while we slept. The ground was fearfully shaken up by shell fire, and the constant rain kept the earth so loose that it resembled sodden loam and quite defeated our attempts at revetting.

Our shooting was chiefly over the Ligny-Thilloy sector, but we did a good deal over to the left round Le Sars and the famous Butte de Warlencourt. Occasionally we turned right, in the direction of Le Transloy, and we amused ourselves at the ends of shoots by emptying guns into Bapaume, which was just within range.

Our usual O.P. was in the old Switch Trench, S.W. of Flers. It was one of the least forward O.P.'s we ever had, being 3,000 yards from the front line, and only a little way in front of the Battery.

The Fourth Army's advance had now been definitely held up on this line. At the end of October, XVth Corps went out, being relieved by Ist Anzac Corps, and we passed under the command of Brigadier-General Frazer; and about the same time, too, we were transferred to 3rd H.A.G. (Lieutenant-Colonel Hanna).

The Australians were pleasant fellows to deal with. Our F.O.O.'s and signallers were frequently up with them and we had a line to Battalion H.Q., although we never succeeded in getting a good forward O.P., owing to the nature of the country. Still, it was valuable experience for everybody, and the signallers in particular were settling down to their work and proving themselves to be a really jolly lot of fellows. A good story is told of a signaller from Yorkshire. This man—T., say,—was detailed to accompany the O.C. to an O.P. the whereabouts of which T. knew. The O.C. led the way, T. following close on his heels. After they had done several miles the O.C. turned to T.

and asked how much further it was to the O.P. T. replied that he could not say as he had lost his bearings hours ago! "Were you not told to take me to the O.P.?" said the O.C. "Yes, sir," replied T., "but aw thaw't tha' know'd seeing tha' walked i' front!"

In many respects we did pretty well by being under the Anzac Corps: we received an almost unlimited supply of engineering material, and we were able to start a rather ambitious dug-out scheme, which, as is often the way, was never completed. We had splendid rations, and frequently a double supply of rum!

We did not get any very severe fighting, although we kept up a steady fire, occasionally firing as many as 500 rounds per day. Appendix E shows the tremendous number of rounds fired in this position.

On the night of October 3rd, the Battery was rather heavily shelled for a time. One of No. 3 gun's dug-outs was hit and Gunner Kershaw was killed. Great credit is due to Corporal (afterwards Sergeant) Hansell, in charge of No. 3 gun, for the good example of coolness and bravery which he displayed on this occasion. This shelling was repeated on the night of the 8th; another dug-out was blown in by a shell, the occupants, Gunners Metcalfe and Senior, being killed. These three were our first casualties, and their loss was keenly felt by everybody.

On the morning of November 13th we put down a heavy bombardment on our front in support of the attack which was being launched in the Ancre sector just north of us—the beginning of the famous Battle of the Ancre.

We moved out of this position on the night of December 1st, and proceeded to the village of Bonnay, near Corbie, feeling very pleased at the prospect of a good clean up and a rest. While we were there Battery Sergeant-Major Lovett left us to take a commission, and Sergeant Napper became acting B.S.M. in his stead.

Prior to the move we had a change of Ammunition Column. Our Column, under Lieutenant Blackstone, A.S.C., went to 67 Siege Battery and their Column, under Lieutenants Howell and Creery, A.S.C., came to us. This fine Column remained with us till the end of the war and looked after us well.

CHAPTER IV

COMBLES

[DECEMBER, 1916—MARCH, 1917]

At this stage the British Army was extending its front southwards by taking over more of the French Line; and it was not long before we were told to get ready to move into the XVth Corps to join the 6th Heavy Artillery Brigade (Lieutenant-Colonel F. H. Metcalfe) in order to cover the portion of the new line between Sailly-Saillisel and Clery sur Somme.

The Brigade H.Q. was at Combles, and the position selected for us* was in the valley below Savernake Wood, and about half-mile S.W. of Combles. It was at least half a mile from the nearest road; and, after a reconnaissance, it was decided that we could get the guns up only by dismantling them at the Plateau railhead and sending up the pieces in trucks on the light railway which passed close to the Battery position.

Accordingly, on December 10th an advance party, consisting of Lieutenants Allen and Richardson and ninety-eight other ranks, was sent up to prepare the position, and to construct a railway siding connecting it to the main Decauville line. No dug-outs were available, and so camouflaged tents were put up against the side of the hill. These were to provide accommodation for the Battery until it was possible to find time to build more reliable and less conspicuous shelters. The ground was covered with snow and we were in for a very miserable and cheerless time.

We were all very grieved, too, to lose our O.C.—Major Sladen—who had formed and trained the Battery in England, and brought it through its first trials in France. He fell ill and had to be invalided to England on December 18th.

---

* Sheet 62c, B. 3c Central.

Lieutenant Wood took charge of the work at the Plateau, and the guns with their respective detachments were sent up to him in turn. The trucks were very small and the great cumbersome 8-inch howitzers had to be completely dismantled—i.e., the wheels, carriage, gun, and buffer separated—before they could be loaded on the trucks. When the first gun had been dismantled and loaded it was sent off with its detachment to the Battery position. No more trucks were available and work on each gun had to be held up until the original lot of trucks had been returned. A powerful crane and other gear were available at the Plateau, and all went well there. At the Battery, however, the task of unloading and reassembling the parts was one of extreme difficulty, as they had only a seven-ton gyn, the various pulleys and tackle, some handspikes and levers, a collection of wooden blocks, and some poor rope. Further, the men had had no training in this kind of work ; in fact, out of the whole Battery—officers and men—only four could be found who knew anything about it—Sergeants Napper and Loker and Bombardiers Coull and Butler, G.F. Great credit is due to these men for getting the work done so successfully.

The weather conditions were appalling and it was a heart-breaking task. Twice during the process of mounting one of the guns, when the piece was slung in mid-air, the rope snapped just as the carriage was being pulled into position to receive it—thus more than undoing the day's work. Still, in spite of such disasters we made steady headway with our job. The first gun left Bonnay for the Plateau on the 12th and was registered on the 21st ; all four were in position and ready for action on the 25th.

Except for the difficulty of moving in, the position was an ideal one. We were right under the hill and quite secure from ground observation and from balloons. All ammunition came on the light railway right up to the guns ; and, in due course, we were able to construct excellent dug-outs on the side of the hill, obtaining all the necessary timber from the wood.

We had in the Battery a number of experienced miners. They mined into the chalk on the hill and constructed large galleries, supporting the roofs with pit-props. Later, we were able to obtain quantities of " Hessian canvas," and with this the walls of these dug-outs were covered : doors were fitted to the entrances and a stove (made out of an oil drum) was fitted in each, thus converting them into quite " desirable residences."

Until these were completed officers and men had been sleeping either in tents or in holes in the ground, under a few sheets of corrugated iron ; and this during a period of very severe frost which lasted for about three weeks. On occasions the temperature, even in our sheltered valley, fell to 1°F. (31° of frost), and one day, when it went up to 16°, we felt it was getting quite warm ! The dug-outs for the detachments on the guns were poor. They were hurriedly constructed on our arrival and consisted of shacks of corrugated iron and sandbags let in to the side of the hill. Later, in order to strengthen them, an outer roof, with an air space of a foot or so, was constructed of large tree trunks laid horizontally, and resting on the hill-side.

When the work on the dug-outs was well advanced it became possible to spare men for the construction of a permanent B.C. post and telephone exchange. Two holes were dug along the side of the hill and in each of these a large " elephant shelter " was erected so that they were in line with one another and separated by a layer of chalk three feet thick ; through this a hole was bored so that telephone messages could be passed from one shelter to the other. In the far end of each an opening was left to serve as an entrance, the remaining space being boarded up and sandbagged, and a trench was dug leading down to each entrance. Chalk was then thrown into these holes to cover the shelters to a depth of about five feet. About a foot above the ground level a " shell-breaker " of iron rails was fixed, and this was finally covered with lumps of turf and brushwood. A wooden floor was laid, and tables, shelves and a stove fitted by Wheeler Nicholson and Gunners Wilcox and Inglis, thus converting them into the most luxurious dug-outs we had yet possessed. In all subsequent positions we endeavoured to build our B.C. post and telephone exchange more or less on this pattern.

Meanwhile we had been joined by our new O.C.—Captain C. P. Heath, from 66 Siege Battery. He had been in England attending a B.C.'s course at the time of his appointment, and it was not until January 17th that he was able to return to France to take up his new duties. He immediately set to work to overhaul the organisation of the Battery, and it may be of interest to note the final distribution of officers and N.C.O.'s :—

Commander: A./Major C. P. Heath.
Captain C. E. L. Phillips.

Right Section:

Lieutenant K. F. Allen.
Second Lieutenant E. G. Richardson.

A. Sub.	*B. Sub.*
Corporal Randall.	Sergeant Loker. Bombardier Darby.

Left Section:

Second Lieutenant S. R. Wood.

C. Sub.	*D. Sub.*
Corporal Hansell. Bombardier Mauchlin.	Sergeant Jack. Bombardier Burns.

Signallers: Second Lieutenant D. J. Walters.
Sergeant Lockley.
Corporal Kemp.
Bombardier Stewart.
Bombardier Todd.

A./B.S.M.: Sergeant Napper.

Q.M.S.: Quartermaster-Sergeant Hawkins, M.M.

Sergeants Wade and Unsworth were both doing duty as B.C.A.'s at the time, but they left to become officers shortly after Major Heath's arrival. Both were highly efficient and extremely pleasant companions.

The chief interest during this period lay in the work done at the O.P.'s. The time of year and the weather were unsuitable for aeroplane work, and altogether only twenty-four rounds were fired in collaboration with aeroplanes. Nevertheless a lot of shooting was done, and in nearly every case was controlled by our own officers at the O.P.'s. Colonel Metcalfe took a keen interest in these shoots, and he saw to it that all officers spent most of their spare time in learning the country in front of them and in locating O.P.'s suitable for observation on particular points. A large number of reconnaissances were made with this object in view, and in these Second Lieutenant Wood did particularly good work. On one occasion he made a very valuable reconnaissance from the front line south of Bouchavesnes. The line there was not really continuous and the infantry manned it in more or less isolated posts, and it was only with great difficulty that he made his way from post to post on account of the nearness of the enemy and the activity of the Hun snipers. On another occasion, in February, 1917, he made a similar reconnaissance of an extremely dangerous portion of the line just north of this, a task which he would have been thoroughly justified in abandoning as impossible. It was some time after the thaw had set in: the trenches were in a beastly state: in many places they had fallen in and were full of sticky mud. This gave the Hun snipers such opportunities that normally there was no movement by daylight in that part of the line. Many times one of the party got so firmly stuck in the mud that it was a most difficult job to get him out again. Gunner Falk was one of the unfortunates, and he could be freed only by pulling him out of his "waders," which had to be left in the mud while he continued the journey in his stockinged feet. This is typical of the conditions under which O.P. work was carried out in those days.

Many O.P.'s were discovered and the two most suitable were selected for "Brigade O.P.'s" to be manned continuously; each battery taking its turn to provide the necessary officer and signallers.

The northern O.P.—Peter*—was in a communication trench south of Rancourt, and about 700 yards from the Hun lines. We were made responsible for the construction and upkeep of this post. The work could be done only at night as the enemy had the place well under observation. The framework of a triangular "pillar-box" (designed by the Major) was constructed in the Battery by Gunner Inglis and covered—except for a loophole for observation purposes—with "expanded metal." This was taken up to "Peter" one night and a slot dug in the side of the trench. The cage was fitted into this with the loophole facing the enemy, and the roof just below the top of the parapet. A piece of corrugated iron was nailed on the top of it and covered over with clods of earth so that there appeared to be no break in the parapet. Second Lieutenant Walters and a party of men, including Gunner Inglis, were sent up to do this job. A period of severe frost had just begun; the ground was like iron, and the digging of the slot was a great labour. However, the post was completed and all traces of the work covered up before daybreak.

---

* C. 2D 0.8.

A few nights later another party consisting of the miners, Bombardier Branch (afterwards Sergeant), Gunner (afterwards Corporal) Jackson, W., and the brothers Chapman (gunners), began the construction of a mined dug-out underneath the O.P. It was very hard work. The ground was still hard with frost and all the timber had to be carried up from the Battery, a distance of nearly four miles; also, they soon got down to the chalk and the greatest care had to be taken to hide the "spoil." In about three weeks they completed a splendid dug-out about twenty feet under the earth, and to which there were two entrances.

The southern O.P.—"Arthur's Seat"*—was a tin shack built into the side of a trench on the high ground on the road well south of Rancourt. This gave a general but rather distant view of the enemy country in front of Bouchavesnes.

The manning of these O.P.'s was by no means pleasant. They were frequently heavily shelled: it was bitterly cold there at nights; and when the thaw came, the trenches became so full of sticky mud that the journey to and from the O.P. became extremely exhausting.

The O.P. party usually consisted of one officer and two signallers. They had to take rations with them for twenty-four hours. It is said that the best people always carried the rations in one sandbag; the various items such as tea, sugar, etc., being kept separate by a series of knots tied in the bag. The contents would be arranged somewhat as follows. At the bottom of the bag came the tea: then a knot: next the sugar, followed by another knot: next the butter and a knot; and last the bread, jam and tinned stuff. Carelessness in tying the knots caused endless trouble. On arrival at the O.P. it might be found that perhaps the tea, sugar, and butter had entered into an unfortunately intimate alliance; or perhaps the jam would take it into its head to come out of its cardboard "tin" and spread itself over the bacon and tea.

Normally the party left the Battery early enough to enable them to reach the O.P. about dusk, when they took over, and the outgoing party handed over the log-book and gave them any information of importance. Most of the observing was done by the officer, although during the night the signallers would each take a turn. There was

---

*C. 8A, o.8.

nothing much to do until daybreak, except to look out for S.O.S. signals and to report to the Brigade any serious shelling, with the direction from which the shells came. During the day-time, on the other hand, there was plenty to do: the Battery would probably be firing and the F.O.O. would be required to control the shoot if the target were within his field of view: also, he kept a look out for any movement or signs of work in the enemy's lines. The signallers manned the telephone and it was their business to repair any breaks in the line. They missed no opportunities of preparing a meal, and very wonderful affairs some of these meals were. In these days we possessed a Primus stove — a "genuine antique." It leaked very badly and air got into the petrol vapour. Consequently it burnt with a series of rapid explosions, making a noise rather like a Ford car! When on its worst behaviour it would explode rather violently at intervals and upset whatever was being cooked at the moment.

It was the custom to take up water in petrol cans, while the petrol was taken up in old water bottles. On one occasion the outgoing party handed over to the relieving party a petrol can and a water bottle, containing water and petrol. The new arrivals set about making some tea. The old Primus was soon exploding merrily, and all went well for a time. Then the officer—who was up in the O.P. —heard most excited noises coming from the dug-out below and one of the signallers shouted to him: "Oh, sir, the water's on fire!" He rushed down, and indeed the water *was* on fire! The fire was extinguished and after investigation it turned out that the signallers had been boiling the contents of the petrol can, and their predecessors had kept their *petrol* in this! This was not the only disaster. The next day, these same signallers—Gunners Wickenden and Hebblethwaite—decided to heat up a "Maconochie" for dinner. The Primus was by now on its very worst behaviour, and it took nearly two hours to get the tin hot, and they were all ravenously hungry when at last it was announced that "lunch was ready." It was with some impatience that they opened the tin. Imagine their horror when they found that they had been cooking a tin of Maconochie marmalade!

In February we did many shoots on the German trenches along the edge of St. Pierre Vaast. These could be observed only from an infantry post in our front line, and this could be reached only under cover of darkness. The difficult problem of communication was solved by connecting the O.P. to the line at "Peter," about 800 yards away. The cable had to be laid down in the open and in full view of the enemy. This was done by four or five signallers in charge of the Battery Signals Officer. They set off early in the morning to reach "Peter" a few hours before daybreak. There they quickly set about their business, and having split up into two parties, disappeared into the pitch-black night to lay two separate cables over the open to the O.P. Machine guns fired incessantly at points along the line: guns flashed in the distance: here and there shells crumped, sending splinters and mud in all directions; then there were the Very lights, which with the occasional crack of a sniper all helped to make the whole thing eerie and uncanny. Further, it was a difficult job to keep one's direction and turn in just at the right point in order to strike the post; while there was always the fear of missing it altogether, or of running up against a patrol. To increase the chances of keeping the line through, the two cables were connected laterally at various points so that even if some parts of it were shot away there still might be a circuit.

This O.P. was again used on February 13th for a shoot on a trench in front of St. Pierre Vaast Wood. The Major and Lieutenant Allen manned the O.P., with Corporal Tapping in charge of the signallers. Early in the morning the line was badly cut by shell fire and had to be repaired. It was a very difficult and risky job, as part of the line ran over the open. However, the linesmen pushed on with their usual grit, and after some considerable time, the line was put "through" again. Corporal Tapping—a very gallant fellow who was always to the fore when there was dangerous work to be done—was in his best form; while Corporal Stewart and Gunner Hebblethwaite, the linesmen stationed at "Peter," did an exceptionally fine piece of work in making their way along the whole line from "Peter" to the O.P. in broad daylight.

The infantry subaltern in charge of the post was distinctly alarmed by this activity on our part; but he appears to have lost his sense of proportion when he sent the Major the following note: "For the safety of this post and of the whole line I implore you not to show yourselves so much above the parapet!" Corporal Tapping was the chief cause of this: he was

MAP TO ILLUSTRATE O.P. WORK.

COMBLES POSITION.

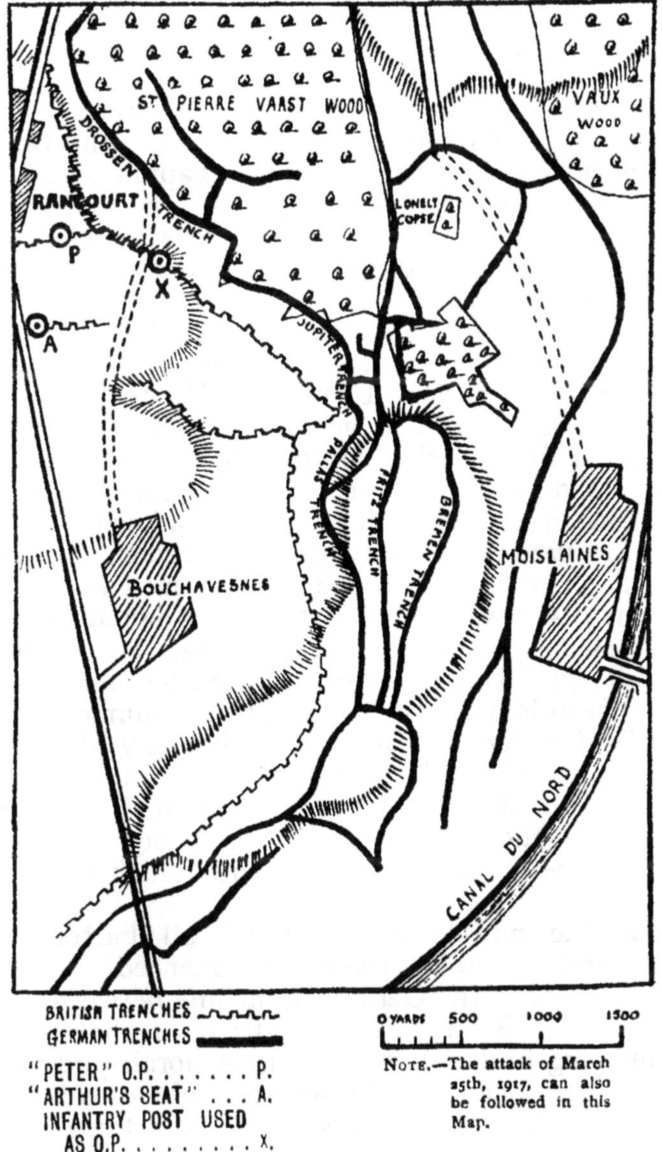

NOTE.—The attack of March 25th, 1917, can also be followed in this Map.

moving about all over the place, and he simply could not be kept in the trench. Later, the Hun shelled the post, and almost immediately Tapping was wounded in the arm. The six infantry men in the post occupied a little shelter of waterproof cloth in the trench, while our party took the best cover they could between a low traverse and two boxes of bombs! A shell hit the waterproof shelter, but, fortunately, all except one of the infantry men had moved away. As soon as darkness came the O.P. party came down the line with Corporal Tapping, who insisted that there was very little wrong with him, and left him at the dressing station feeling that he would soon be fit enough to return to duty. A few weeks later we were all saddened to hear that he had died in hospital from septic poisoning. In him the Battery lost a very brave soldier and one of its most interesting fellows.

On another occasion, Lieutenant Walters with Gunner Wickenden and another signaller manned a post in the front line a little farther south in order to range our guns on a point in the enemy's front line. They had an eventful day. Our first round fell short and missed the O.P. by only a few yards! Shortly after this the enemy retaliated by shelling the post. All the infantry men were wounded, while our party were more fortunate, a damaged telephone being their only casualty. Corporal (afterwards Sergeant) Kemp did fine work in repairing the line under fire. The line had been laid in the open as the communication trench was full of water, and he worked his way along the line right up to the O.P., which was in a very exposed position. All these instances are quoted to give some insight into the life of the Battery signallers, and to show the fine spirit and courage with which they did their work.

About the middle of February, all batteries—Siege, Heavy, and Field Artillery—commenced a series of bombardments of the German front line between St. Pierre Vaast and the Somme River, a front of about 5½ miles; the aim being to destroy the enemy's morale and to deceive him as to the point at which we were subsequently to make a minor attack. It is interesting to note that, to observe on one of these tasks (some enemy trenches near Feuillaucourt) we used an O.P. south of the Somme, using a line over ten miles long. These daily bombardments continued with varying intensity right up to March 25th, when the XVth Corps launched their attack in front of Bouchavesnes. (See map on page 37.)

The object of the attack was merely a local one, i.e. : "To gain all ground from which the enemy can obtain close observation of the Bouchavesnes Valley and the valley that runs N.W. from it towards Rancourt." This meant, roughly, the capture of Pallas Trench and Fritz Trench (the German front and support lines) on a front of about 1,200 yards—an advance of about 300 yards. The attack, if successful, would have a more important result still for us, as gunners, in that it would enable us to get a good view of the Moislaines Valley, which hitherto had been hidden from us.

The attack was carried out by the 25th and 24th Brigades of the 8th Division.

Our task was as follows :—

Time.	Task.	Rate of Fire.
5.15 a.m. to 6.15 a.m. (Phase I.)	Jupiter and Jupiter support C.10A, 22.72 to C. 10A, 05.98. Special attention to Trench junctions and M.G. emplacements at C. 10A, 25.90 and C. 10A, 30.80.	5.15 to 5.25 a.m. "Intense," 5.25 to 6.15 a.m. "Medium."
6.15 a.m. onwards. (Phase II.)	Jupiter Alley (three guns). Junction of Hill Trench and Link Avenue (one gun).	10 rounds per hour.

Intense Rate = one round per gun per minute.

Medium Rate = one round per gun per two minutes.

This area was very difficult to see as most of it was in dead ground. The Major decided to send Second Lieutenant Wood to "Peter," from which parts of the task could be seen, and in particular the junction of Hill Trench and Link Avenue.

The attack commenced at 5.15 a.m., supported by a barrage of the Heavy and Field Artillery ; and all objectives were captured without much loss. We fired 256 rounds with success, as far as could be judged.

Later in the morning, Captain Phillips, accompanied by Corporal Maddock, volunteered to go up the line in search of information. It was more or less of a joy ride on their part : we had no real business there at that time, as separate arrangements had been made by the Heavy Artillery H.Q. for liaison officers to work with the infantry.

They arrived on the captured ground before the position had been consolidated, and while the hostile barrage was still on it. They were frequently under rifle fire, and once the periscope carried by Corporal Maddock was hit by a sniper. In spite of these incidents Captain Phillips went along the whole of the captured line and brought back a detailed report of the view obtainable from various points. The best O.P. he found was at the end of a bombing sap at C. 10c, 6.4. From this point he located three hostile batteries which could plainly be seen in action in the valley below. This reconnaissance was the only good one made that day, and Captain Phillips received a well-deserved letter of commendation and thanks from the Corps Commander for it.

Captain Phillips' account of the O.P. sounded so attractive that the Major got permission from Brigade to attempt a destructive shoot on these batteries on the following day.

Communication promised to be difficult. The distance from Battery to O.P. in a straight line was about four miles: no buried cables were available; and, further, the forward part of the route was being heavily shelled by the Huns. A large party of signallers, under Sergeant Lockley, was sent up early to connect Arthur's Seat to the new O.P., and so provide a line through to the Battery: while Captain Phillips accompanied the Major to the O.P.

The view was indeed wonderful. One seemed to look down on Moislaines and the surrounding country as from an aeroplane or balloon; and there, clearly visible below, were the enemy batteries. The guns were in covered pits, and between two of them a sentry could be seen. The farthest battery (five pits) had the mouths of the pits covered with gate-like "screens." Suddenly from behind each pit a Hun emerged to remove the "screen," disclosing the nose of the gun. Then five flashes, followed by five reports, and five shells came screaming over and burst in the communication trench behind. Imagine the impatience to strafe these blighters! The nearest battery was the only possible target. This had two emplacements just east of the Canal, north of Moislaines. The range from our Battery was just 10,000 yards, and it was just possible that we could reach it. [The maximum range of the

8-inch Mark V. howitzer, when new, is 10,500 yards, and ours were not new.]

The Major telephoned the target to the Battery. Then shortly after came the report: "Number one gun ready, sir!" from the telephonist. Then "Fire No. 1," from the O.P. Over she came, but burst short. "Up 2°," from the O.P. Still the rounds were short. At last the maximum elevation was reached, and still we were short, not even over the Canal. Alas! there was to be no sport that day. A strong head wind was blowing, and the temperature was low, and these adverse conditions just made all the difference. The enemy was in no hurry to get away, and we tried to reach him on two subsequent days, but fortune was always against us.

Shortly after this we received orders to move by sections into a new area, and on March 13th the Left Section guns were put "out of action," prior to being taken down the line.

Meanwhile the Right Section kept up a steady fire to mask the withdrawal of half the Battery.

On the 16th the Germans began their withdrawal to the Hindenburg Line, and on the 17th they were out of range. The Right Section then packed up and left Combles for the Plateau on the 24th.

We had spent a happy time at Combles and we were all sorry to leave. There had been few casualties, and most of these were cases of sickness.

CHAPTER V

The Battle of Arras

[March—July, 1917]

The guns of the Left Section had been dismantled on March 13th and sent down to the Plateau, and on the 15th they were mounted again ready for the road. That evening the remainder of the section—the 1st Echelon—arrived at the Plateau by light railway and loaded its stores on to the lorries, and on the following day we set off on our long trek. Major Heath was in command, and he had with him Second Lieutenants Walters and H. J. Goodwin, and Battery Sergeant-Major Banfield (Battery Sergeant-Major Lovett's successor). Second Lieutenant Goodwin had joined us from England on February 13th to take the place of Second Lieutenant E. G. Richardson, who had done extremely good work with us until he left to join the R.F.C., in which Corps he was serving when he was subsequently fatally wounded.

The route and stopping places were most carefully worked out for us by the Staff, as there were many batteries on the road, all moving north. At night all the villages were full, and their squares and streets were packed with guns, caterpillars and lorries. There was a touch of romance and mystery about the whole move, and it was very pleasant to think that this crowd of guns was on its way to give Fritz a nasty knock in some other part of the line. On the fifth day we arrived at Avesnes le Comte, which we had reached by the following stages :—

	Billets at	Distance travelled.
1st day	Plateau	—
2nd day	Rivery	30 miles.
3rd day	Villers Bocage (north of Amiens)	7 miles.
4th day	Gezaincourt (near Doullens)	10 miles.
5th day	Avesnes le Comte	15 miles.

A typical day on the move began with an early breakfast in order to get started as soon as possible. The officers and men travelled in the lorries with the exception of a small party which travelled as a guard on the guns. The lorries kept together as a column with the slowest lorry in front to set the pace, while the caterpillars and guns followed as a separate column at about three miles an hour. The A.S.C. officer had a busy time dashing up and down the line on his motor cycle to see that all was in order; occasionally leaving one column to go on ahead to reconnoitre the road, or to go back to see that all was well with the caterpillars and guns.

The Major always went on as early as possible each day to our destination. There he interviewed the Maire or Town Major and endeavoured to reserve the best billets for us before representatives of any other batteries arrived. On arrival the men were taken to their billets and a meal provided for them, after which they were free to do as they pleased. Of course, the chief centres of attraction were the estaminets, but occasionally members of the fair sex—technically known as " bits of fluff "—caused a considerable flutter in the hearts of our younger and more romantically-inclined members.

We arrived at Avesnes le Comte on March 20th. There we learnt that we were bound for the Arras sector to join 32nd H.A. Brigade (Lieutenant-Colonel Jacob) in the VIth Corps.

We were to do counter battery work, and so a position, as close up as possible and 2,800 yards from the front line, had been selected for us* in the gardens of some private houses right in the middle of the town of Arras, near the Place Vauban. No movement was allowed in Arras during the day, and so when we moved up on the 21st we arranged to arrive at Arras after dusk, the guns being left to follow more leisurely and to reach us the following night.

It was quite a novelty in our experience to come into action in a large town, with real streets and many undestroyed houses, and to have a few civilians living near us. We were billeted in the houses, whilst close by there were canteens and estaminets, and the whole thing was a pleasant change after the muddy, desolate, and cheerless Somme sector.

---

* Sheet 51B, G. 27d 7.9.

THE ARRAS POSITION.

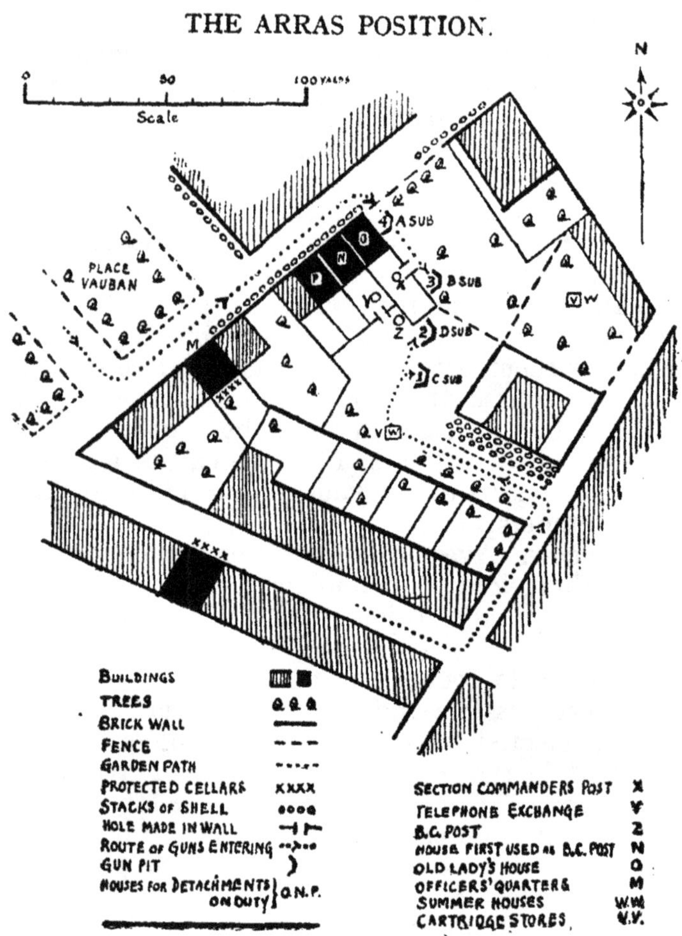

The proposed position was a most interesting one and presented all sorts of difficulties. It consisted of an orchard and a lawn containing numerous flower beds, with a frontage for all four guns of only about sixty-five yards, so that we should be cramped for room. Two pits had already been dug in the orchard to take 6-inch howitzers, and the Major decided to work on these to prepare them for the Right Section guns, taking care from the outset to hide the pits well by putting up " camouflage " netting under the trees. There were many borders of shrubs and plants in the orchard, and other similar detail which would show up well on an aeroplane photograph, and it was vitally important that these should not be destroyed. Accordingly, on the following evening all these plants were pulled up and removed, to be replaced early next morning when the guns were in position, and all caterpillar and gun-tracks had been obliterated. Later, thin wire fences were put up to prevent people straying from the " official " paths and trampling on these borders.

The actual pulling in was extremely difficult—the ground was soft and the gun-wheels had to be kept on planks. Further, the caterpillars had no room to manœuvre as there were so many trees, and, in fact, one or two had to be cut down at the roots—to be planted again when the caterpillars had gone. This scrupulous care to avoid giving the position away was maintained to the end, and the Germans, in spite of the keen vigilance of their 'planes, never suspected that the orchard contained four such monsters. Later, on the first day of the attack, our F.O.O. captured a German counter-battery map on which our position was marked only as a harmless orchard, even though many of the British battery positions had been more or less correctly located.

The second echelon, under Captain Phillips, arrived on March 30th, and they pulled in their guns on the following night, taking the same elaborate precautions to hide themselves.

The men lived in cellars which were protected by thick layers of bricks and stones covering their more vulnerable parts. The B.C. post and the telephone exchange were first in one of the summer houses, then in a bedroom of one of the houses overlooking the Battery, and finally in a dug-out. [See plan of position.]

We were not allowed to fire for some days ; nevertheless

the men had plenty to do. Each night hundreds of rounds of ammunition came up, until at last we had 3,600 rounds. There was very little room in the position, and the shells were stored in long lines stretching along the streets round about Place Vauban. They were placed two deep, right up against the walls of the houses and thus hidden from aeroplanes. All this shell humping meant very hard work for Lieutenant Howell and his A.S.C. Column. Later, during the bombardment, an officer and twenty O.R.'s of the Hants Regiment were attached to us to assist in this work.

A tremendous number of batteries had been concentrated in this sector: in the VIth Corps alone there were nearly 140 siege guns, including one 15-inch and four 12-inch howitzers; and on April 4th the preliminary bombardment began. The attack was to be on a large scale, and it had many possibilities. This will be seen from the following extracts from Operation Orders:—

1. The VIth Corps has been ordered to take part in operations ot the Third Army which have for their object the turning of that portion of the enemy's defensive line which runs from Arras to St. Quentin.

2. The following Corps are co-operating in the attack: XVIIth Corps on left (i.e., attacking Vimy Ridge), VIIth Corps on right, XVIIIth and Cavalry Corps concentrated in rear to exploit the success of either attacking Corps.

3. The objective of the VIth Corps is Monchy Le Preux.

4. The attack will be preceded by a four days' bombardment (days V, W, X and Y).

(Note.—Another day, "Q" day, was subsequently added between X and Y. "Z" day was to be the day of attack.)

On W/X and X/Y nights the bombardment will be of sufficient intensity to prevent the enemy repairing his trenches and bringing up his supplies.

* * * * *

7. The principal work of Heavy Artillery on Z day will be counter battery work.

It is interesting to know that on the southern flank the attack was to be aimed at the "Harp"—a very elaborate system of defences near Tilloy—which formed the northern pivot for the German withdrawal to the Hindenburg Line. North of this there had been no voluntary withdrawal.

It was our task to fire on certain enemy batteries, which were grouped mainly (1) in "Battery Valley" (E. and N.E. of Tilloy); (2) in the Scarpe Valley; and (3) behind

Orange Hill. Occasionally, too, we bombarded villages such as Feuchy, Fampoux and Athies.

Owing to the heavy bombardment it was not possible to observe these shoots, but an attempt was made to use aeroplanes to correct any inaccurate shooting. A programme was worked out by the Staff giving each battery periods of fifteen minutes each day during which it was to fire alone on its bombardment tasks. An airman flew over the targets during this interval and signalled the position of each burst with reference to the target. The angles for each gun were then corrected so as to bring it on to its task, and for the rest of the day the guns fired without observation, further corrections being applied only if a change in the weather conditions demanded them.

Although we were firing hundreds of rounds daily yet there was little for the F.O.O. to do except to check the line of the guns occasionally, and to keep a close watch for movement, etc., in the enemy's country. We manned at least one O.P. each day, the most useful one being Vulcan.* This was a tall factory chimney about 150 feet high near Arras Station. Inside it were rungs by which the F.O.O. ascended to a platform at the top where a good view could be obtained of most of the country as far back as Monchy. It was a very "windy" business climbing that chimney, particularly as many of the rungs were loose. Unfortunately just before the bombardment commenced one of our field batteries in action just behind it hit the chimney and brought it down.

Another chimney stack—Ann†—was also used, but it was not so high as Vulcan and the view was not so good. On one occasion the Major and Bombardier Crumpling were there, sitting on a platform near the top of the chimney peacefully eating their lunch. Suddenly there was a loud crash, followed by a shower of bricks and dirt. In the scramble down the chimney the lunch was lost, and they were very annoyed to find that the "incident" was due to one of our own 60-pounders which had taken a piece off the top of the chimney.

The best forward O.P.—known as X 49‡—was a concreted room in a ruined house near Arras Cemetery, and about 700 yards from our front line. From this a good

* Sheet 51B G. 28C, 80.25. † G. 28B, 0.9. ‡ G. 29B, 2.7.

view was obtained of the front system of trenches, of Orange Hill and of parts of Monchy.

The enemy artillery became more active during the bombardment period, and on the first day ("V" day) he shelled Place Vauban rather heavily with 5·9's. Splinters from one of these hit the B.S.M. and B.Q.M.S., who were standing at the corner nearest the Battery. Battery Quartermaster-Sergeant Hawkins was seriously wounded, and much to everybody's sorrow he died the same day. Battery Sergeant-Major Banfield, though badly hit in two places in the leg, refused attention until he had seen his friend, "the Quarter," safely taken away on a stretcher. He, himself, went off to "Blighty," and did not return to us, although it is good to record that he recovered.

On "Z" day we were detailed to provide the Brigade F.O.O. to man O.P. X 49 for the attack, and to run a line forward as closely as possible after the infantry's advance. Lieutenant Walters was selected for this, and at 2 a.m. he set off from the Battery position with a party of six signallers and Gunner Morton (who had volunteered his help), armed with cable drums, signalling lamps, picks, shovels and other gear. On reaching Arras Station they got into a tunnel which took them up in safety to the Cemetery near the support line. This tunnel was a wonderful affair, lit up by electric light; and leading off from it at various points there were huge galleries filled with hundreds of infantrymen snatching a few hours' sleep before the battle. Here and there, too, were the headquarters of many of the units taking part in the attack. The party reached the O.P. about 4 a.m. All was quiet until 5.30 a.m.—zero hour. Then, in an instant, the whole front burst into tremendous activity, and the sky became lit up with the flashes of guns. Shells were bursting all over the German lines, and his S.O.S. rockets were going up at all points. Simultaneously, our infantry, which that day included such famous divisions as the 3rd, 12th, 14th, 15th, 21st, 30th, and 56th, left their trenches and following closely after the Field Artillery barrage, soon captured the enemy's first line. The enemy barrage was five minutes late, and after an hour or so, it slackened off, and finally stopped as his batteries were captured. The infantry swept all before them that day. The enemy offered very little real resistance, and our casualties were slight—a splendid tribute to the way the gunners had done their part of the job.

MAP TO ILLUSTRATE POSITIONS IN THE ARRAS SECTOR, 1917.

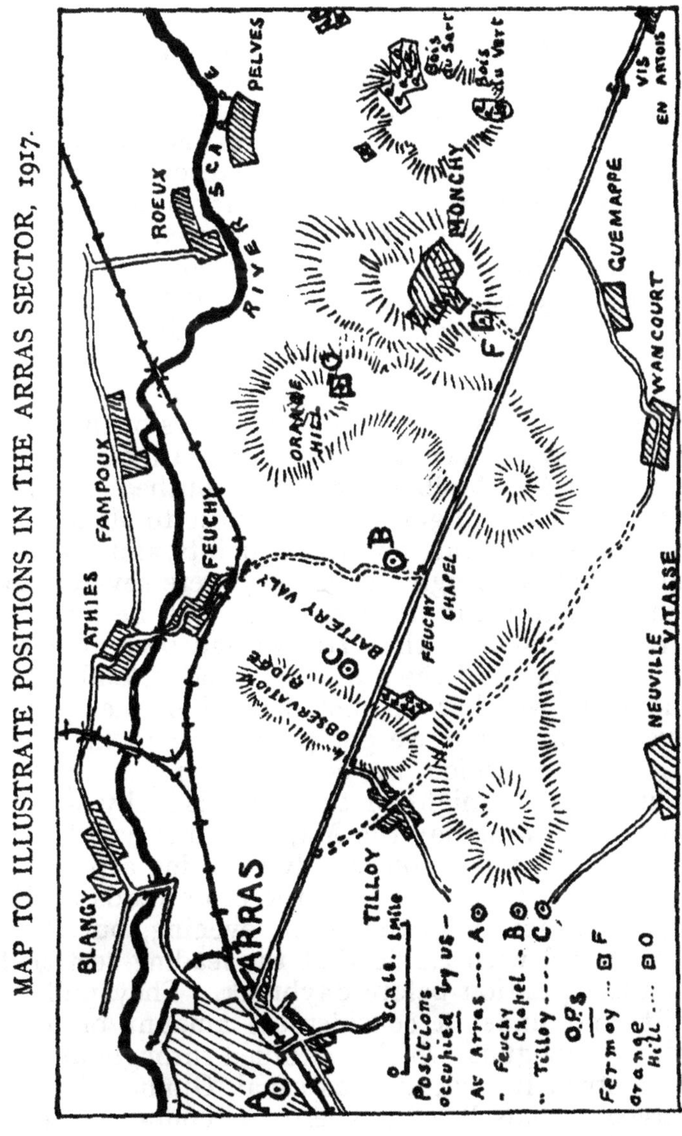

The F.O.O. and his party advanced close behind the infantrymen and reached the next ridge before the Huns there had been mopped up and while bombing was still on. An infantry Sergeant-Major with twenty or thirty prisoners on his hands borrowed a signaller, armed only with a D. III. telephone, to conduct them to the line of infantry in the rear. Later in the morning our party got into a German dug-out just after the Germans had vacated it, finding their steaming breakfast there quite untouched—and miserable food it was, too! Before dusk our infantry were on Orange Hill, and had captured the Wancourt-Feuchy lines—an advance of about 5,000 yards. On our flanks also, big advances had been made (including the capture of Vimy Ridge by the Canadians) and large numbers of prisoners and guns had been taken with very slight losses to our troops. Without a doubt we had achieved our biggest success since the days of the Marne.

On the following day Lieutenant Wood took over at the O.P., and with Bombardier Todd pushed forward to Orange Hill to an old gun pit quite close to Monchy. The Battery continued firing on distant points, and the advance was continued, although the cavalry were severely cut up in an attempt to break through at Monchy Le Preux.

On the afternoon of the 11th we had been told to stop firing even though all the guns were loaded, and it became very doubtful whether we should be able to empty them. However, at midnight we got permission to fire them off into Guemappe, which we could just reach at extreme elevation. On the night of the 11th, Monchy was taken, and on the following day the Major went forward to reconnoitre for another position, finally selecting a point on the road about 200 yards north of the cross roads at Feuchy Chapel. We moved up that same evening, but the roads were so packed with traffic that the leading section failed to reach the position before daybreak. They pulled in in daylight and under a considerable amount of fire from 77-mm. and 4·2 guns, which continued throughout the day. The men stuck it well, and, as usual, Gunner W. Jackson and Sergeant Hansell set a cheery and courageous example to all. The first two guns were in position at 1.30 p.m., and registered before 3 o'clock ; while the other two, which had come up later, were ready for action at 6.30 p.m.

The neighbourhood was rather crowded with guns. Immediately behind us, about seventy yards back, was a battery of R.H.A., and on their right, 116 S.B.: 137 S.B. were about fifty yards away on our left: just south of the cross roads two more siege batteries; while in front and further up the slope there was a long line of field guns. They were all in the open, and unprotected, although subsequently most of us built sandbag walls round our guns. Further, there was no cover from aeroplanes, and so we put up "camouflage" netting over each pit, but this was a failure and rather tended to make the position more obvious.

On the first night the gun detachments slept in shell holes under their waterproof sheets, and the officers slept in the B.C. post—a shell hole with a gun cover for a roof! The remainder of the Battery went about 500 yards back to an old German position where there were splendid dug-outs. This position we retained as a "billet" for men off duty. Later, we were fortunate to get hold of some German dug-outs near the Battery for the gun detachments and these were invaluable. One of these was a large dug-out in a quarry near the guns, in which officers were quartered, and which also provided sleeping accommodation for two gun detachments.

The enemy appeared to know all about the concentration of batteries in this area. From the very beginning he shelled the place almost incessantly; either harassing with 77-mm. and 4·2's, or trying to destroy some of the batteries with heavier shell like 8-inch or even 11-inch.

There was very little cover above ground, and whenever we had a rest the personnel, except for the aeroplane sentry, retired to trenches close by for cover, ready to rush on to the guns whenever "action" was given. These periods of rest, however, were short and infrequent, as the guns were kept hard at it, firing hundreds of rounds each day. A glance at the appendix will show the tremendous work done by the gunners in these trying days. In the month of April we fired off more rounds (5,600) than in any other similar period in the whole history of the unit.

All this was done under the almost constant harassing fire of the enemy. Occasionally he did a "destructive shoot" on us. Perhaps his most successful effort was on April 21st, the opening day of our bombardment prior to the second big attack on this front. At 4 p.m. on that day, two batteries, 8-inch and 4·2-inch howitzers, began a "destructive shoot" on us, being ranged by aeroplanes, whose signals and observations were picked up by our wireless operators, Tomsett and Hardy. The batteries, well ranged in a short time, soon rained shells into the position. One of the first rounds sent up a big dump of shell with a terrific explosion, and soon our cartridge dumps were ablaze: the pits were hit many times, and the camouflage covering and the gun covers, too, were all on fire, and the scene and noise are indescribable. Behind us were three tanks, laden with petrol and ammunition, and they too were hit, and burned in a most fearful blaze.

We had been compelled to evacuate the position at the outset, and this was done with only one casualty—Gunner Manning, whose leg was broken. When it seemed that all had been cleared we were horrified to see dimly in the smoke-enveloped position, a figure endeavouring to put out a burning cartridge dump. This turned out to be Captain Phillips, imperturbable as ever, and it was only with difficulty that the Major called him away. The bombardment ceased at 6.30 p.m., by which time about 200 rounds of 8-inch and more than this number of 4·2's had been fired at us.

We returned rather warily to the position, and the Major, with Staff-Sergeant Band and Fitter Hill, held a minute inspection of the guns. Only one gun was completely "knocked out"; another was out of action on account of a damaged spring case, but the fitters soon put this right. The other two were quite sound except for a few splinter holes and scratches.. The position itself was in a horrible mess: everything had been burnt and everywhere there were burnt cartridge cylinders. The B.C. post and signal exchange—holes in the ground with corrugated iron roofs—had been smashed in, and most of the signalling equipment had been destroyed.

We got busy clearing up the position. The guns were repaired; the B.C. post, wireless station and telephone exchange were crowded into a dug-out underneath the road on the left of the guns, and although we had been ordered by Brigade to keep away from the position that night, we had three guns ready for the opening of the bombardment at 6 a.m. next morning.

In this bombardment we fired mainly on counter-battery targets, occasionally joining all the other batteries in prearranged ten-minute concentrations on Plouvain,

Vis-en-Artois, Roeux or Boiry Notre Dame—villages in German lines.

On April 23rd, the infantry of the Third Army attacked again with the idea of advancing about 1,000 yards on our immediate front to prepare for another advance later to the line Biache—Boiry Notre Dame—Rohart Factory. The attack was but partially successful, however, and only a few of our objectives were taken.

The attack had commenced at 4.45 a.m. and we continued firing right up to the afternoon, expending nearly 580 rounds. The enemy shelled us at intervals with 5·9's and 4·2's, and the latter got well on to us on occasions and wounded four men, one of whom—Gunner Robson—unfortunately died in hospital. The attack was resumed at 4 p.m. on the 24th by the 15th, 29th and 12th Divisions, but still without success. For this our orders were "to stand by" to receive targets from aeroplanes and to fire under their observation—N.F. work. Accordingly at 1 o'clock a plane sent us a target—a German battery—and we were quickly ranged on it, receiving 9 Z's (within twenty-five yards), 2 Y's (within ten yards), and 20 O.K.'s (direct hits), and we continued firing up to sixty-four rounds. Earlier in the day a Bosche plane had ranged a 5·9 gun on to us, and the signals and observations could be distinctly heard on our wireless set.

Meanwhile the F.O.O.'s and signallers had been having an equally bad time. The O.P., established by Lieutenant Wood on Orange Hill on April 12th, had been pushed on to Monchy on the following day by Lieutenant Allen. This was a most unhealthy spot, being shelled all day by all sorts of stuff. He established the O.P. in a house on the north side of the village, but it proved quite impossible to keep the line through. In those days, a linesman's job called for infinite grit and pluck. When a line went "down" at any time of the day or night it was his business to go out to find the break and repair it, no matter how severe the shelling. On occasions the shelling might be so bad that the line was cut as rapidly as the linesman could find the breaks and repair them. The signallers, all of them, took their turn as linesmen, and in every case the same spirit of courage and devotion to duty was shown, while a few like Gunners Inglis and Allan seemed to enjoy it. On the night of the 12th some of those splendid fellows laboured under these heartbreaking conditions to try to put this O.P. line through to the Battery. The whole O.P. party, Lieutenant Allen and Gunners West and Burdock, struggled for hours on this line, until finally West and Burdock were wounded—the latter fatally—and they had to be taken under cover until daybreak.

Soon it became obvious that it was hopeless to attempt to maintain an O.P. in Monchy, and the Major, with Signallers Gardner and Keeley, set off in search of a more suitable post. Monchy was being strafed as usual, and Keeley was severely wounded in the head by a splinter, his tin hat saving his life. An O.P. was found near an old German dug-out on the south side of the village, just in the rear of our front line. The old O.P. line was deflected to this point via an old concrete machine-gun post (T.B.) on the Battery side of the village. To prepare for an emergency, visual communication, too, was established between the old O.P. on Orange Hill—T.A.—and T.B., and arrangements were made to connect T.B. with the O.P. by runners if necessary. The Major manned the O.P. that day.

A few days later Lieutenant Wood, with Signallers Markham and Lewis, went off to the O.P. The Huns had advanced during the night, and day was breaking as they arrived. A Hun sniper, who had spotted them, fired three rounds on the party at close range. Two missed, but one hit Lewis in the groin, and Lieutenant Wood pulled him into a shell hole and attended to him ; while Markham, who was some way behind, crawled back to T.B. There was no hope of escape for Lieutenant Wood and the signaller. They were kept huddled in this hole till dark, being fired at and shelled at intervals throughout the day. At dusk a small party of signallers, under Lieutenant Walters, went over from T.B. and brought them in. This long exposure had been too much for the wounded man and he died in hospital on the following day (April 20th).

We were having no luck with our O.P., and we had to move it again, this time to a point in a trench on the high ground just south of Monchy. This O.P.—Fermoy—was shelled pretty severely most days, and communication was still as difficult as ever. The view from it was a good one and, fortunately, we were able to continue to use this O.P. for the rest of our stay at Feuchy Chapel.

On the evening of the 24th, the day of the unsuccessful attack by the 29th, 15th and 17th Divisions, Lieutenant Goodwin and Signaller Hill were returning from the O.P.

View of Monchy, looking East.
(Immediately under the Crucifix can be seen the concrete shelter used by the Battery for visual signalling.)

and had got within half a mile of the Battery when a shell burst behind and killed them both. They were found later in the evening by Bombardier Todd. This was not the only disaster, for earlier in the day Gunner Lamb had been killed in the Battery position by a premature from the battery just behind us. These gallant fellows were buried side by side in the cemetery at Arras on the following day.

We had good reasons for believing that all this " hate " from the Hun was being well repaid, and with interest. We shelled the enemy's battery positions and billets almost incessantly, and the observations of aeroplanes and our F.O.O.'s all showed that we were getting well on to our targets and " putting the wind up Fritz." On one occasion at Fermoy, Lieutenant Wood spotted a hostile battery of two 4·2-inch guns firing from the road near Vis-en-Artois. The flashes were plainly visible, appearing to come from some mounds of newly-turned earth. We got permission from Brigade to fire at this battery. The guns were immediately silenced, and about twelve men were seen hurrying away from the position.

The Battery, as a whole, kept in good spirits in spite of the rough time it was having. The wits kept their ends up, and the cooks—down at the billets—had an unlimited fund of good stories which they retailed to the signallers and gun crews when they came down for their evening meal. Gunner Willmot always had a cheery song to sing at nights ; while Gunner Hartshorn—the inventor of that hardy perennial, " Hartshorn stew "—had a stock of rumours to suit all tastes.

On one occasion the detachment of No. 4 gun were sitting in their emplacement yarning, while No. 3 gun, firing to a flank, pointed almost directly over them. There was a lull in the conversation which gave the pessimist his chance : " My word, we wouldn't 'alf cop it if No. 3 'ad a premature." A pause—then Tully, optimistic as ever, shattered him with the reply, " Oh, it might be a dud, after all ! "

The A.S.C. Column, under Lieutenants Howell and Stevens, continued to serve us well. They were always cool and cheerful about their work, although the Battery, the approaches to it, and particularly the cross roads near by, were constantly shelled. They never allowed our ammunition supply to be delayed, and frequently brought the lorries up under shell fire; while the officers always remained with us until the last lorry had been unloaded and had got safely away.

On May 1st our artillery began a bombardment prior to an attack on the 3rd by the Fifth, Third and First Armies. The objective on the Third Army front was the line Fontaine—Les Croisilles—Cherisy—St. Rohart Factory—Bois du Vert—Bois du Sart—Plouvain Station—Square Wood, an advance of from one to two thousand yards.

As usual our task was the bombardment of battery positions. In addition, we joined all the other batteries of the Heavy Artillery in prearranged 10-minute bombardments of certain villages. These "crashes" (as they came to be called) must have had a very demoralising effect on the enemy. In our Corps there were about 150 heavy guns, and the rate of fire was one round per minute per gun; that means that about 150 rounds per minute (for ten minutes) were poured into the unfortunate village, suddenly and without warning enveloping the whole place in smoke and brick dust. Our F.O.O. reported that during a "crash" on Vis-en-Artois a big fire was caused which burned for an hour and a half.

At intervals during the bombardment the enemy retaliated by shelling us and all the other batteries round about Feuchy Chapel. One night he hit a big dump of petrol tins near the Arras-Cambrai road, causing a tremendous blaze, which, to say the least, distinctly alarmed our signallers sleeping in some dug-outs on the roadside and almost underneath the dump!

The attack on May 3rd was timed to take place at 3.45 a.m., just before daybreak. This was a typical zero day, always full of bustle and excitement for the gunners, and it is worth while here to give some account of the work done in the Battery on such a day. Long before zero hour the detachments on duty were awakened by the sentries and were soon busy preparing for a hard day's work. On each gun most of the crew set to work to fuse shells, while the limber gunner—the gun's nursemaid—took off the muzzle and breech covers and went round with his oilcan getting the gun into thorough fighting trim. Soon the Major and his B.C.A., the invaluable Corporal Slinger, had worked out all the angles for the Battery, and had written out on a separate slip of paper the angles and bombardment programme for each gun. These were taken round to the guns by the Battery officer whose job it was to look after the work at the guns. About fifteen minutes before zero orders were given to load the guns and lay them on their initial targets, the officer going round to each gun in turn to check the angles on the sights and to verify the actual laying of the guns. Meanwhile voices could be heard in all the other batteries round about as they too were getting ready for the fray. Soon all was ready, and the whole place became still and quiet again, except that at intervals the silence was broken by the voice of the Battery officer as he shouted out the official time. A minute before zero hour came the order, " Stand by for gun fire." Then, after a pause, " 30 seconds," " 20 seconds," " 10 seconds," " Battery—fire ! " Immediately there was a deafening roar as every gun thundered into action, and all along the front—right up to the far end of Vimy—the flashes of hundreds of guns could be seen, as it were stabbing the darkness with darts of fire.

Rapid fire was maintained for some time, and by 10 a.m. we had fired over 300 rounds. The rate was gradually slowing down, and by the end of the day we had sent over 630 8-inch shells—nearly sixty tons—into the enemy batteries allotted to us as our task. In the afternoon extra targets were sent to us from the Brigade, and at 4.20 our F.O.O., who had spotted a Hun battery in action, ranged us on to it. The battery was soon silenced, and some horses and limbers were plainly seen galloping away from the position. At 4.30 a plane called us up to fire a few rounds on a battery officially known as I.D. 19, and one of our tasks in the morning's bombardment. Out of five rounds fired for the airman three were unobserved, one O.K., and the other a Y. (i.e., within ten yards), which seemed to indicate that we had been well on this target all day.

The infantry attack, however, was unsuccessful. The enemy had abandoned his front trenches and established posts in shell holes. These had been difficult to locate, and, manned by machine gunners, they had held up our men.

After this, both sides gradually quietened down in this Sector, although we continued to do occasional counter-battery shoots of 150 rounds or so ; and on the 10th we left a guard on the guns and moved out to camp in Arras for four days' rest, after one of the roughest periods in the history of "135." At the end of his account of this period, Major Heath writes : " Throughout this trying time all the officers gave me the greatest possible help and support, and they were always cheerful, courageous and willing. Captain Phillips took his turn with the subalterns in all duties, and by his steadiness under shell fire set a splendid example for us all. Lieutenants Allen and Wood did most of the important O.P. work ; and frequently, after a hard twenty-four hours at the O.P., returned to do duty in the Battery. Lieutenant Walters, as signals officer, did admirable work in keeping our many lines and signalling arrangements in good order, and, in addition, took his turn at Battery work and occasionally helped at the O.P. Second Lieutenant Goodwin, who was unfortunately killed, also did his bit well.

" All the signallers—every single man—did well, and it would be invidious to single out any one for special praise. Sergeant Kemp, N.C.O. in charge of the Section, was a great help and did splendid work.

" Of the gunners, it is difficult to mention all who did well, but Sergeant Hansell, Sergeant Napper, Corporal Branch, Bombardier Jackson and Corporal Mauchlin stand out.

" Staff-Sergeant Band and Fitter Hill did good work, being always on the spot to repair any damage done to the guns ; while Corporal Slinger was invaluable as a B.C.A."

On May 15th, after four days' rest, we returned to Feuchy Chapel, but only for a short stay. On the following night we pulled out without any feelings of regret, and moved into the Corps on our right—VIIth Corps. A small party of men, under Lieutenant Wood, were left behind to collect some stores and to clear up the position. While at work next day they were heavily shelled ; a cartridge dump was blown up and Corporal Clemence severely wounded. Sergeant Hansell again distinguished himself by his coolness and bravery. Regardless of the danger, he attended to the wounded man and carried him off to a place of safety. On the following night the Battery pulled into a position* on the slope of a high hill and just south of Heninel. We did not enjoy this part of the move : it rained hard most of the night and we were all soaked to the skin ; and as there were very few dug-outs or shelters, many of us remained wet for some days.

---

* Sheet 51B, T.4B, 3.6.

There is nothing much of interest to record of this position, although we did a considerable amount of firing and assisted in one or two minor attacks. We moved out on the night of the 29th, and received a very lively send-off from the Hun. It was a clear summer's day and a battery on our immediate left, which was also to move out, brought up their lorries early in the afternoon and pulled out in full view of two Bosche balloons. Of course, this folly had the inevitable result. At 5.30 the Bosche opened fire on them with a 5·9 battery, but by this time our neighbours were ready to move and quickly disappeared down the road, leaving us to pull out and load up our platforms under heavy fire which lasted until after we had gone. We got the guns away early, but few things are more beastly for a battery than to have to pack up lorries crowded together on a road which is being shelled. We were exceedingly lucky to get away without casualties, and, as we passed through Henin just after midnight, it was almost pleasant to hear the regular "crump-crump" of the shells as they burst on the hill far behind us.

In the course of the night we arrived in the position near Tilloy,* which a party of men, under Lieutenants Allen and Wood, had for some days been preparing. The guns were pulled in without incident before daybreak.

We remained in this position (about 700 yards behind our old Feuchy Chapel position) for just over a month. O.P.'s were manned at Fermoy, and later, in a railway cutting (South O.P.) just south of Guemappe, and about 1,000 yards behind the front line. We did counter-battery shoots (of 100 rounds or more) almost every day either with aeroplane or balloon observation, and on June 14th we fired over 500 rounds to neutralise enemy batteries during a successful attack by our infantry.

We did a lot of work on the position and had completed some very fine mined dug-outs, including a combined B.C. post and telephone exchange, and had taken great trouble to camouflage the position, when we were warned that we should be moved early in July into the XVth Corps. The 1st Echelon, consisting of Lieutenants Walters and Wood, Battery Sergeant-Major Falconbridge and the Left Section, pulled out on July 3rd, and was billeted in Arras for the night *en route* for the railhead to entrain for Dunkirk.

---

* H. 32d, 8.8.

They were followed by the second half of the Battery about five days later.

We all enjoyed our stay at Tilloy. The Hun left us in peace and life on the guns was not too exacting. There was a reasonable amount of leisure for everybody. We went so far as to train a tug-of-war team with a view to challenging neighbouring batteries, but we had to move before a match could be arranged. Lieutenant Curtis had joined us at this position, also Battery Sergeant-Major Falconbridge and Quartermaster-Sergeant Chapell.

CHAPTER VI

NIEUPORT

[JULY–NOVEMBER, 1917]

In July, 1917, the Fourth Army moved up to the Coast Sector to take over from the French and Belgian Armies the portion of the line between Dixmude and the sea. This line ran northwards from Dixmude along the Yser Canal to St. George's, thence east of Nieuport to the sea, keeping on the east side of the canal and at distances from it varying from 500 to 1,000 yards. It appeared to be our intention to attack in this sector in conjunction with the Navy, provided the attack then in progress in the Ypres Sector met with sufficient success to make it worth our while. The line was held by the XVth Corps, with their H.A. Headquarters at Oost Dunkerque, about seventeen miles east of Dunkirk.

The Battery left Arras on July 7th, and on the following afternoon arrived at Dunkirk, where they were met by Major Heath, who had travelled up by car. The guns and caterpillars were unloaded before nightfall and sent off to Zeepanne; and later in the evening the personnel were taken in lorries, borrowed by the Major, to the H.A. Rest Camp—a number of bell tents round Groot Boogarde Farm, about 1½ miles south-west of Coxyde.

Along the coast between Oost Dunkerque and Nieuport, there is a strip of sand about a mile broad. It is very uneven ground consisting of high dunes and deep hollows. Behind a range of dunes, from seventy to 100 feet high, known as the Blekker, a position* had been selected for us by the 34th H.A. Brigade (Lieutenant-Colonel Liston-Foulis), to which we had been posted on arrival in the XVth Corps; and already another battery had begun to make two pits for us, working under coverings of yellow canvas erected over each pit to hide them.

---

* Sheet 11 : R. 28D, 38.

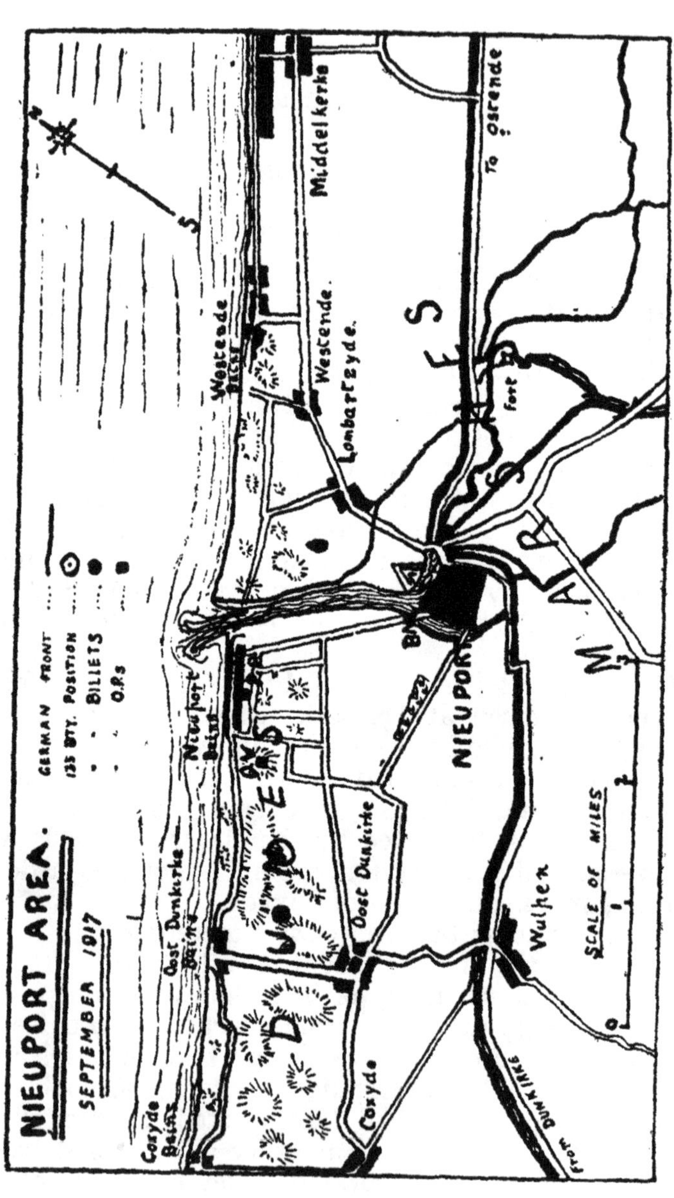
NIEUPORT AREA.
SEPTEMBER 1917
GERMAN FRONT
135 BTY. POSITION
BILLETS
O.Ps
SCALE OF MILES
0
1
2
Coxyde Bains
Oost Dunkirke Bains
Nieuport Bains
Westende Bains
Middelkerke
Westende
Lombartzyde
Oost Dunkirke
Coxyde
NIEUPORT
Wulpen
Fort
To Ostende
From DUNKIRK
DUNES
MARSHES

The task of pulling in our heavy guns over a long stretch of sand promised to be a difficult one. Two routes were possible. By coming in from the coast road we should have a comparatively short stretch of sand (about 350 yards) to cover, but it meant climbing over a high ridge of sand. This was rejected in favour of the alternative, namely, to pull in from the Oost Dunkerque—Nieuport road over about a mile of sand, which was flat for most of the way and held together in places by grass. To lessen the weight of the guns and so to minimise the risk of disaster in crossing over the sand, it was decided to take out the piece from each carriage and to move it up separately on a 9·2 gun-wagon. This dismantling of the guns was carried out at Zeepanne by a party under Lieutenant Wood. They had one serious mishap which resulted in our losing a very capable and stout-hearted Sergeant-Major, Battery-Sergeant-Major Falconbridge. While one of the " pieces "—weighing a few tons—was being held up by the gyn, the rope holding it snapped and the " piece " fell on the B.S.M.'s foot. Some bones were broken, and he had to be evacuated to the base, and, subsequently, to England.

The men not required at Zeepanne went up to the position on July 9th to construct two pits, lay platforms and to unload the lorries on the road at a point whence the stores could be taken up by Decauville railway to within 200 yards of the pits. This work was carried out under constant fire, as the areas round Coxyde and Oost Dunkerque and all the roads were shelled continuously. To make matters worse, 500 rounds of ammunition were unloaded for us at this same point, and we were kept hard at it all night pushing trucks up and down the line. The enemy fire became more severe at night and a lot of gas shells were fired into the dunes. This gas worried us so much that work had to be stopped for a time and gas helmets worn. All this activity was the preliminary to an attack next morning on our line between Nieuport and the sea. Except for the Divisional Artillery we had very few guns in position, while the French gunners had moved out a week or so earlier. The enemy attack was overwhelming, and there was little support for our infantry. They put up a splendid fight: north of Lombartzyde they were almost annihilated, and the enemy, capturing our front system of defences at this point, pushed our line back over the canal. South of Lombartzyde the attack was repulsed and we retained our original line and the town of Nieuport.

On the following night the guns came up, two caterpillars being used to pull each " load " from the road to the pits. In this way all four " loads " were taken to within a few feet of the platforms without difficulty. This was all the caterpillars could do as there was a steep slope up to the pit and a ridge on the far side of it. The guns were covered up, and the caterpillars sent back to Zeepanne, while we spent the rest of the time covering up their tracks in the sand. It was too risky to attempt any work on the guns in daylight, and so, after a few hours' rest, the men were employed in " shell humping " ; some in pulling up truck loads of shells on the Decauville, and others in the laborious business of carrying or rolling them, one at a time, from the line to the gun pits—a distance of about 200 yards.

We had only one gyn, and it took us two nights to mount the guns and pull them on to their platforms. On the second night the caterpillars came up to take away the 9·2 carriages. There was some delay, and they left us only a short time before daybreak. We were hurrying to cover up the gun pits and to obliterate the caterpillar tracks when a Hun bombing plane, returning from a raid, spotted us, and, flying very low, dropped a number of bombs all round us, wounding three of our men, Gunners Crewe, Hughes and Mitcheson.

That night the Right Section, under Captain Phillips, arrived at the Rest Camp. They came up on the following day to prepare two pits about 300 yards in rear of the Left Section. There was a fairly safe track from the road in Oost Dunkerque Bains to these pits, and it was decided not to dismount these guns but to take them straight into the position. The guns came up on the night of 14/15th, and, using two caterpillars to pull each gun over the sand, we got them safely on to their platforms before dawn.

There were very few dug-outs in the vicinity. Near the guns there were two narrow concrete passages which served as temporary shelters for the gun detachments; the only other dug-out, built of wood and protected with tree-trunks and sand, was used as the B.C. post with the telephone exchange and wireless station in wooden huts near to it. The remainder of the Battery was housed temporarily in a group of wooden huts about 500 yards

VIEW OF THE COUNTRY N.E. OF NIEUPORT.
Taken from an aeroplane.

south of the guns. These were often shelled and were very unpleasant quarters. As soon as we could obtain the necessary material we set to work hard to build shelters for ourselves in what appeared to be the safest spots.

Within a few weeks we were able to move our " billets " to elephant shelters constructed in the sand about 400 yards behind the rear guns, one shelter being allotted to each detachment and one to the signallers. The men were fairly comfortable here, although an infantry track close by attracted a certain amount of harassing fire at night. One of these shells hit A subs.' shelter when it was full of men sleeping side by side. The door was blown in and the whole place filled with dust and smoke. When this had cleared away a candle was lit and it was found, much to our sorrow, that Gunner Davis had been killed and three others wounded.

For the dug-outs on the guns we had the help of a party of sappers from 256 Company R.E. (Tunnelling Company). Galleries were constructed under the sand dunes and fitted with two entrances. These were the only really safe dug-outs we possessed, as without skilled labour it was impossible to build anything more than splinter-proof shelters.

The gun pits, too, required a great deal of attention as the sand was always slipping down and filling them up. We built revetments of wood round each pit, but these never succeeded in withstanding the tremendous pressure of the sand. The most successful revetment was constructed of barrels filled with sand and strengthened with stout balks of timber ; but barrels were difficult to obtain, and then only by " scrounging."

The O.P.'s. in this sector were close up to the front line : they were most interesting, and we made good use of them. The most popular one—Beer Emma—was a strong concrete tower built inside a house in Nieuport, which stands very high above the surrounding country ; and from this O.P. one looked down on the trenches and fortified houses in and around Lombartzyde, and obtained a good view of the enemy country as far back as Ostend on a clear day. Flashes of hostile guns could be picked up quite easily, and occasionally we saw movement on roads in the back area. We manned this O.P. almost continuously, and Lieutenants Allen and Wood, who did most of the forward observation work, got to know the country well.

Sometimes we manned an O.P. just in front of Nieuport,

near the bridges connecting the town with our front system. These bridges attracted a lot of fire, and it was a very unhealthy post to man. The O.P. was a tower inside the ruins of an estaminet—the Café de Lys.

Other O.P.'s used by us were "P.P."—a house in Nieuport Bains within a few yards of the sea beach, and quite close to the front line; "O.V."—the top of a high sand dune near "P.P."; "V.C."—a house south of Nieuport on the road to St. Georges. We had lines to most of these O.P.'s and did many shoots from them, often using cross observation with much success.

The signallers, as usual, had a strenuous time. The line to B.M., in particular, caused endless trouble and was very difficult to maintain on account of the incessant shelling of Nieuport and its approaches. On August 19th the shelling was particularly heavy, yet our line to B.M. was never out of action for long. This was due to the untiring and fearless way in which the linesmen, Bombardier Allan and Gunners Ward and Carrington, did their job. A special report on their work was sent up to H.Q., as a result of which one of them, Bombardier Allan, was awarded the Military Medal.

The following incident is typical of the unconcerned way in which the signallers carried out their work. One day the enemy shelled the B.C. post: shells burst all round it, and after a time one hit the telephone exchange. This was just a corrugated iron shelter in the ground protected by a shell breaker of iron rails a few feet above it. We were none too happy about this shell breaker, and the Major feared the worst when he went along to see whether any one had been hurt. The place was in a hopeless mess: the shell breaker had collapsed and the rails were badly twisted, while part of the dug-out had fallen in. On clearing away some of the debris, he found Gunner Mackay inside the partly destroyed shelter calmly smoking his pipe and busy testing the lines to see how many were "down"!

The guns of both sides were very active right from the beginning. The enemy shelled our trenches, roads and battery positions almost incessantly; while we did long destructive shoots almost every day, either on enemy batteries or on important trench points. We also joined the other batteries on our front in prearranged "crashes" on villages and houses; and we made a nice mess of the Palace Hotel in Westende Bains, which received its share

Street in Nieuport, showing "B.M." O.P.

of these "crashes." In this fierce artillery duel the enemy batteries had a big advantage over us as they were well protected in concrete emplacements and, as a rule, it was difficult to do them much harm.

The following extracts, taken at random from the Battery Log Book, will serve to give some idea of the work done by us :—

"September 2nd.—F.O.O. at B.M. reported a T.M. firing at a slow rate on our front line. We were given permission to engage it at 2 o'clock, and it ceased fire after our fourth round. Altogether we fired fifty rounds at it, obtaining several direct hits, setting fire to their ammunition and causing a small explosion at about 2.20 p.m. and a very large one at 3.30 p.m."

"September 15th.—Shoot on bridge north of Nieuendamme Fort with aeroplane observation. Bridge destroyed by No. 4 gun after thirty-three rounds."

"September 17th.—Lieutenant Wood (at P.P.) spotted machine-gun firing from an emplacement in a shell hole. We fired thirty-three rounds at this, the last round dropping into the emplacement and destroying it."

"September 29th.—Corporal Mauchlin went up to 'Café de Lys' with the Major. They spotted an undestroyed concrete shelter in the German front line. No. 3 gun was turned on to this to show the Corporal how his gun fired. The gun shot well and in twenty-two rounds the side of the shelter was blown in."

"October 24th.—Fired on ammunition dump at Chapelle House. After sixty-third round the dump blew up."

The enemy had not been long in locating the Battery, which was often heavily shelled by him. He did many deliberate shoots on us, causing a number of casualties, including Gunners Kenworthy, Coates and Burgess, who were killed; and once or twice some of the guns were so badly damaged that they had to be sent down to the Ordnance Workshops for repairs. Occasionally the Hun battery got more than it bargained for! Some time in October a 5·9 battery began a shoot on the forward section. We promptly informed our F.O.O. (Lieutenant Wood) at B.M. He, alert as ever, spotted the flashes of this battery in the dunes north of Lombartzyde, and the rear section was turned on to it at once. Salvos were fired and the hostile battery was silenced immediately and did not trouble us again! On another occasion we were doing a

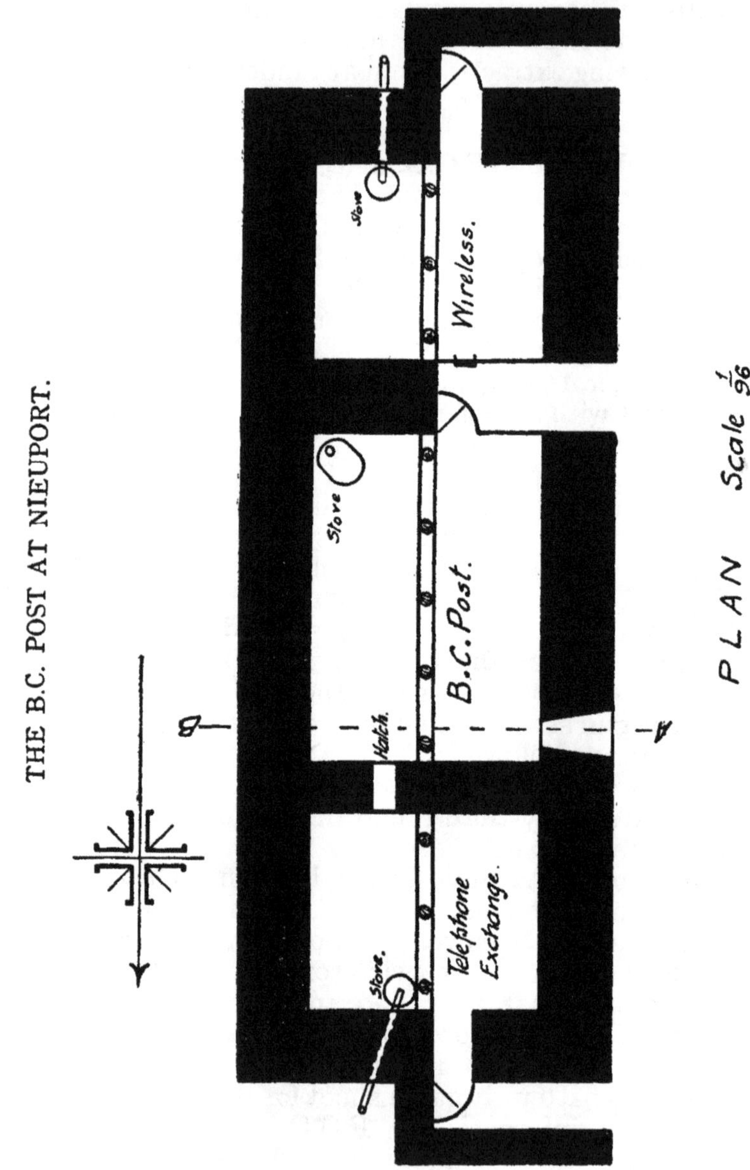

THE B.C. POST AT NIEUPORT.

THE B.C. POST AT NIEUPORT.

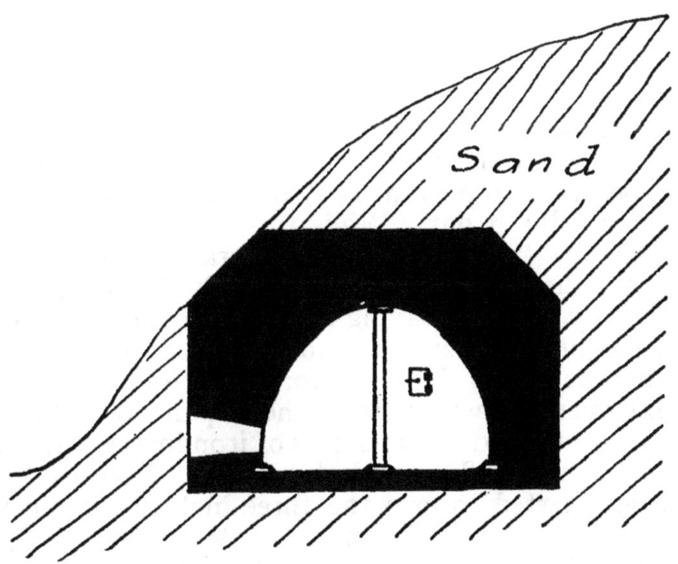

SECTION on A-B
Scale 1/96

counter-battery shoot with aeroplane observation when an enemy battery opened such accurate fire on us that we were compelled to take cover. The airman, seeing our plight, signalled to us to wait while he went off in search of the Hun battery. He turned a 9·2 battery on to it and soon we were able to proceed with our shoot in peace and quiet!

Early in October both sides began to settle down to a more peaceful life and, as we seemed likely to remain in this position, the Major decided to build an elaborate concreted B.C. post, "fitted with all modern conveniences," and containing rooms for the telephone exchange and wireless station. Second Lieutenant W. D. Hooper (who had joined us in July) was in charge of the job, and he had Bombardier Waghorn and Gunner Vernon as his chief assistants. A position was selected for it just south of the Rear Section, in the side of a sand dune, which would afford a certain amount of protection. The task of cutting away the side of the dune was no easy job as great precautions had to be taken to prevent the sand falling into the hole as fast as they dug it out. While this digging was in process the necessary timber, expanded metal, Portland cement, shingle and heavy cupolas were brought up on the Decauville railway, a track having been laid to connect the main line to the site. When the "hole" had been dug a raft of concrete nine inches thick, reinforced with expanded metal, was laid over the whole floor, the expanded metal sheets being turned up and short lengths of iron inserted to make a bond between the floor and the walls. Rod-iron dowels were also inserted to grip the three-inch planks on which the elephant irons were to rest. When the floor had hardened, the cupolas were erected and strutted with heavy pit-props; and the shuttering for the ends and walls fixed. After cutting an opening for a window and fitting up the chimneys, the structure was encased in three feet of concrete reinforced by two layers of expanded metal. Sand to a depth of four to six feet was thrown over this as soon as the concrete had "set." The sides, too, were covered with sand, and grass planted over it so that it seemed part of the sand dune against which it was built. Finally, shelves, doors, tables and stoves were fitted into the rooms, and the whole of the interior painted white. This monumental work had taken six weeks to complete, and altogether 250 tons of concrete had been used. It must have been the finest B.C. post in France, and we were very pleased with ourselves when we moved into it towards the end of November.

Alas! we were not to enjoy the fruits of our labours for long. Within a few weeks we were ordered to move, and it was a very delighted French Battery Commander who took over our position in December. We pulled out on December 6th, and moved by road in easy stages to join the XIIIth Corps in front of Arras.

We had done another hard spell of fighting and we had suffered many casualties. The Battery had done more than its share of good work and all branches had acquitted themselves well. The dispatch riders—Bombardier Purvis, Gunners Butcher and Chapman—will always remember this position, and it required the highest courage and determination on their part to ride along the shell-swept roads at all times and in all weathers.

Lieutenant Reid, Second Lieutenants F. A. Stevens and H. Minns had joined us while we were at Nieuport; and Battery Sergeant-Major Beaumont had come to take the place of Battery Sergeant-Major Falconbridge. We were all sorry to lose Lieutenant Walters, who left us at the end of November to join the 49th H.A. Brigade as their Signals Officer.

It is interesting, too, to record that "leave" began in September, and when we left Nieuport in December all the officers and most of the men had already been on their first Blighty leave.

CHAPTER VII

Vimy Ridge and the German Attack of March, 1918

[December, 1917–March, 1918]

About December 12th, 1917, the Battery, with its equipment of four 8-inch Mark V howitzers, having spent some days on the road from Nieuport, arrived in the Arras Sector. The Battery was posted to the 83rd Brigade R.G.A. (or, as it was then called, the 83rd Heavy Artillery Group), commanded by Lieutenant-Colonel C. S. S. Curteis, D.S.O., which was comprised in the XIIIth Corps H.A., commanded by Brigadier-General L. W. P. East, C.M.G., D.S.O. The move from the coast had been carried out under the supervision of Captain Phillips during the absence of the Major, who was on a course in England.

Two guns, which were to constitute a Rear Section, went into position just west of Maison de la Côte, on the Arras—Bailleul road, while the two remaining guns were pulled into pits formerly occupied by the enemy and situated in Bailleul, a village on the forward slope of the Vimy Ridge.

On December 24th the Battery was joined by one section of the 258th Siege Battery and thus became a six-gun battery. Second Lieutenants T. R. Wood, W. R. Jones and E. Hill came with the new section, together with Sergeants Baldwin and Irvine and about sixty other ranks.

The Rear Section, which had been thus augmented, was in a position bare of natural cover, which made it exceedingly difficult to conceal the guns from aerial observation. For some reason, which was never divulged, the guns were sandwiched alternately between four 9·2-inch howitzers belonging to the 69th Siege Battery. This arrangement led to endless trouble and inconvenience and seemed difficult to justify either from a fighting or administrative point of view: the front occupied by the eight guns was by no means large for four, and there was consequently a danger of both batteries being neutralised simultaneously.

The forward guns were, in the first place, under the command of Lieutenant K. F. Allen, who had with him Second Lieutenants Stevens, Minns, Hill and T. R. Wood, but on the return of the Battery Commander, early in January, Captain Phillips took over command. The two guns were in pits about six feet deep behind a very stout ruin nearly ten feet high. The distance from the German lines (Oppy Wood) was about 3,200 yards, and the ruin itself was under direct observation of the Bosche, especially from the high ground round Crest Wood and Bois-en-T. A canvas screen on iron poles was erected in front of the guns, but we found it very difficult to maintain this intact owing to the enemy's shell fire and the blast of our own guns. There were several excellent dug-outs in the vicinity which helped to render the position tenable. Ammunition was supplied by a Decauville which ran close to the guns.

In addition to manning the rear (" X2 ") and forward (" M ") positions, the Battery was made responsible for the preparation of an alternative position for two guns at " N." The proposition was the construction of two pits on the west bank of a sunken road with overhead cover sufficiently strong to stop a 5·9-inch shell. This was a big task, and required a capable engineer and about fifty men. Second Lieutenant Reid and twenty other ranks were all that could be spared for the work, and this reduced the numbers at the fighting positions to a minimum that was hardly workable.

The O.P.'s in this neighbourhood were the best the Battery ever had, and for long distance and counter battery work they were probably the best on the British front. The Vimy Ridge, round the foot of which the British front line ran, dominated all the country to the east and afforded wonderful facilities for observation. There were three Brigade O.P.'s, No. 3 on the Ridge west of Bailleul, No. 4 about 1,500 yards farther north, and Ajax, which was farther south, being about 500 yards north-east of the Point du Jour. In addition, we had our own O.P. near the new " N " Position, as the Major made it an invariable rule to establish, whenever practicable, an O.P. for the separate use of the Battery. At this period Lieutenants Minns and Stevens did duty alternately as O.P. officers.

About this time a change was made in the system of command of Heavy Artillery. Hitherto, a " Group " system had been employed under which heavy and siege batteries were included under a Group H.Q. according as the tactical situation required. There was thus no permanent command in the R.G.A. corresponding to the R.F.A. Brigade; but the R.G.A. Brigade now came into being, and batteries were permanently brigaded under a Lieutenant-Colonel and Staff. We were fortunate at the time this change in organisation took place, to be included in the 83rd Brigade R.G.A. under Lieutenant-Colonel Curteis, D.S.O.

The Rear Section at "X2" remained fairly quiet throughout the whole of January. The weather was bad and quite unfavourable for observation. The construction of a mined dug-out was commenced under the supervision of Bombardier Jackson (better known perhaps as "Busty"), who was an expert at the job. Later on, this work was responsible for the saving of many lives.

On January 10th the forward position at "M" was heavily shelled. A cellar, used as a dug-out, was blown in, and Gunner Hughes was buried under the debris. Luckily, he was unhurt. The section were out of communication with the rear position all day. News, however, was finally obtained by Gunner McKay, who bravely volunteered to go and find out what was happening. The shelling was continued on the 11th and 12th, and during these days things were very unpleasant. Bombardier Todd (afterwards Sergeant), the N.C.O. i/c. of Signallers, gained the Military Medal for the excellent work he did in his endeavours to keep the line through to the Rear Section.

Early in January information came through that each battery in the Corps would, in turn, go out for a fortnight's rest. The official intimation waxed eloquent as to the benefit which would be derived therefrom. Battery Commanders would be able to get their commands into first-class fighting trim, and the men would have time to realise what a jolly thing war was under such conditions. Every one was immensely pleased, as with the exception of five days at Arras early in 1917, the Battery had been in the line ever since its arrival in France. Joy rags were already beginning to make their appearance, when another circular came from H.Q. This was an intimation to the effect that:—

(1) All guns were to be left in action with sufficient crews to man them in case of S.O.S., and one officer was to be left at each position.

(2) The party at "N" were to continue their work with their officer.

(3) "Young officers" from other batteries in the Corps were to be attached to the Battery for instruction. They were to live at "M" position and act as gun detachment for the No. 2 gun, doing all the duties of gunners.

(4) The remainder of the Battery were to go on rest to Acq.

In spite of this wet blanket the Major hurried off to secure billets. Having arrived at Acq, he was surprised to find that the Town Mayor there knew nothing about any "rest party," and had no billets to spare in any case. He was advised to try Bethonsart. This he did, but the people there seemed as ignorant of a rest party as the authorities at Acq. Finally the only billets available were secured. These consisted of barns without any bunks or straw for the men to sleep on and were not at all comfortable.

On January 15th six officers and 122 other ranks, out of nine officers and 200 other ranks, set out for the "rest." It was raining in torrents and every one was wet through long before the lorries which were to convey the party arrived. They were three hours late. Bethonsart was finally reached at 1 a.m., and when the wretched billets were seen more than one man was heard to wish himself back at the Battery, and the promoters of the "rest cure" to a somewhat more distant clime, albeit a drier and warmer one than the billets!

The next day the usual "rest" training was commenced, and the men were beginning to find life just supportable when, on the 18th, Ordnance notified that two Mark VI howitzers were ready to be delivered to the Battery to replace the Mark V howitzers with which we were armed. Brigade gave orders that these guns were to be put into a new position (afterwards called "S") at Bailleul as soon as possible. Lieutenant Hill and twenty-two other ranks from E and F Sub-Sections went off to carry out the exchange. After this it became evident to every one that the "rest" was a swindle. Parties of men had to go all over the place unloading new guns and looking after the old ones as they came from the Battery to the railhead. It was probably nobody's fault that the replacement of the old pieces took place at this time, but it was very unfortunate that the men should have been led to expect a fortnight's Elyseum.

On January 23rd Major Heath, looking thoroughly fed-up with life, returned to the Battery with Staff-Sergeant Hill and Quartermaster-Sergeant Clarke and helped in the changing over of the equipment. A day or so later the remainder of the rest party came back feeling that they had been badly " had."

" S," the new forward position, was occupied on the night of January 23rd. The two Mark V guns at " M," which, up to then, had been the Forward Section, were pulled out on the 27th, and the personnel from that position went to " X2 " on the 28th. " S," like " M," was on the forward slope of Vimy Ridge, and about 2,500 yards distant from the Hun lines. The two new guns were pulled into old German concrete emplacements constructed for firing west, but capable of being used the other way. These were strongly built with two feet of concrete as overhead cover. On the left front of the guns was a small concrete dug-out which was used as a B.C. post until better accommodation could be found. There were several good mined dug-outs in the vicinity, but they were generally in a bad state of repair. Bombardier Jackson and his party, who were set to the work of repairing the entrances, soon improved matters, and by February 8th had completed their task and connected two dug-outs by mining through a distance of fifteen feet. Bombardier Waughman also did some useful mining work and joined up with an old Hun shaft on the left front of No. 1 gun pit. It was hoped that these precautions would make the position tenable. There was a scraggy row of trees about twenty yards in front of the guns, but this was the only natural cover. We supplemented it by erecting a screen of camouflage, but it became almost impossible to maintain this intact and on several occasions it was set on fire by the flash from the guns.

On February 1st the disposition of the personnel was as follows :—At the Rear Position (" X2 "), Lieutenant Allen (vice Captain Phillips, on leave), Lieutenant Curtis (signals officer), Lieutenants Hooper and Stevens (section officers), and Lieutenant T. R. Wood, Battery Sergeant-Major Beaumont and Battery Staff, A, B, E and F Sub-Sections.

At the Forward Position (" S "), Major Heath, Lieutenants S. R. Wood and W. R. Jones, with C and D Sub-Sections (Sergeant Hansell and Sergeant Burns).

On January 28th the Forward Section fired for the first time from its new position. The Major registered the guns

One of the German Gun-Pits used by the Battery at "S" Position.

on the southern corner of Crest Wood and observed the shoot by standing on the top of one of the gun pits. To the surprise of everyone the enemy did not proceed to shell the section out of existence, although he must almost have been able to see the guns with the naked eye. On February 1st a very successful destructive shoot was carried out on a hostile battery officially known as "UZ7." One O.K. was obtained and a large explosion was caused. The same afternoon, with the help of the Sound Rangers, a destructive shoot was carried out on "CB 16," which was shelling the Battery. The Bosche was silenced after ten rounds had been fired, and five O.K.'s were recorded during ranging. The Counter-battery Staff were so pleased with this result that they asked the Major to lunch, on which occasion they exhibited the sound ranging films of the shoot.

Some amusing shooting took place on February 4th. The Hun was shelling Bailleul Village when, standing by the guns, the Major spotted the flashes of the enemy battery in Crest Wood. Fire was at once opened on a point which, from the map, seemed to be the position of the active battery. Six rounds sufficed to shut him up, but another Bosche gun to the right took up the challenge. The section switched on to this fellow and the third round from No. 2 gun caused an explosion in the wood. The Hun opened fire again in the evening at about 5.15, but was once more promptly silenced. Anything in the nature of a destructive shoot on the enemy battery was scarcely practicable, as observation for line only was possible; the wood being in that part about 400 yards in depth, range would have been most difficult to establish.

On February 9th the enemy shelled Bailleul all day long with 5·9-inch and 4·2-inch, and from this day onwards he became very active, bombarding the vicinity of the section with a large number of gas shells.

About this time the threatened German offensive was beginning to occupy the mind of the G.O.C., H.A. Instructions were received that the guns were to be fought to the last man, and that the two machine guns and the rifles in the Battery were to be kept ready at hand to be used in case of emergency.

On February 16th a hostile battery of three 4·2-inch howitzers carried out what was evidently intended to be a destructive shoot on the position at "X2." He succeeded in knocking the place about, destroying some ammunition and slightly damaging one gun. It was decided that this indignity should be avenged by a combined effort on the part of ourselves and 69 S.B., the 9·2-inch battery that shared "X2" position. Observation was to be carried out by aeroplane. The plane called up at 10.12 a.m. on the 17th, just as the Hun was again opening fire and doing damage to some ammunition on the Decauville in front of the position. We started ranging, and having completed, "69" was in turn ranged by the plane. All guns then stood by for orders to open the fire for effect. A few seconds later eight guns belched forth at the wretched 4·2-inch, who quickly gave up the unequal contest and presumably provided a job for the German Ordnance Department, as he was not heard of again for some time.

A few days later, a party of six "young officers" from various batteries in the Corps joined the Forward Section at "S" for instruction in aeroplane ranging and O.P. work. It was a compliment to the Battery Commander to be thus entrusted with the training of these officers, and is evidence of the reputation which the Battery had won for itself.

The work at "N" position was still proceedingly slowly. On February 25th Lieutenant Hooper was sent there to take charge. He was undoubtedly the man for the job, and considerable progress was made after the personnel under his command had been increased by twenty other ranks lent by a neighbouring Brigade. The work, however, was rather more than we could manage at the time, and the scheme was finally abandoned about three weeks later.

A very successful aeroplane shoot, carried out by Lieutenant S. R. Wood, from "S" position on February 27th, greatly offended the Hun, who replied with other of his batteries. During the strafe, Gunner Pacey was wounded. News was sent through to the Rear Section, and Bombardier C. Gricewood, the medical orderly, a splendid fellow who had done excellent work, and Gunner Mackay, who has already been mentioned for his bravery, at once set out for the Forward Section. Unfortunately they were knocked out by a shell while proceeding along the railway cutting, and both died of their wounds on the following day. The Battery thus lost two very gallant men.

On March 2nd the Brigade Commander summoned all his Battery Commanders to a conference concerning precautionary measures to be taken in connection with the

German offensive which it was expected would be launched as soon as weather conditions should make it possible. The chief points decided were :—

(1) If attacked, the Vimy Ridge was to be held at all costs.

(2) The forward sections of batteries were to maintain an ammunition supply of 300 rounds per gun, and rear sections, a supply of 150 rounds per gun.

(3) All telephone lines from the Corps burys to batteries were to be laid in trenches one foot deep as soon as practicable.

(4) As far as possible, arrangements were to be made for cooking food underground and a supply of water was always to be reserved underground.

(5) Rifles were to be kept on the guns and the men instructed in their use. Liason was to be established with the nearest infantry unit to enable the Battery to co-operate with them in defending the position.

(6) Means were to be pre-arranged for the destruction of the guns, if necessary, especially in the forward positions, and holes were to be made in secret places so that the breech blocks could be buried in case of a temporary retirement.

(7) Battery Commanders were to live with their main section and not at detached forward positions.

(8) Exhaustive measures against gas attacks were to be undertaken. All dugouts were to be made gas proof. Gas chambers were to be constructed, and detachments were to be practised in serving the guns in gas masks.

As far as possible the above precautions were taken. The provision of a gas chamber was, no doubt, theoretically sound, but in practice it proved to be of little value. It consisted of a chamber with three compartments. Men whose clothes had become impregnated with gas entered the first compartment, where they would take off their outer clothing. In compartment No. 2, they would have a bath, and after that proceed to the third compartment where a new set of outer clothing would be issued to them ; and for this purpose the Battery was supplied with thirty sets of " spare clothing." A conception so comprehensive might well have included the provision of a seven-course meal and a cinema show after the passage through the bathing chamber in order to minimise the danger of the men taking cold, but this seems to have been overlooked. What was actually happening at this period was that both positions were being shelled with gas night after night. The very ground was becoming thoroughly impregnated so that the nice clean boy emerging immaculate from one end of the gas chamber would just have time to look at the weather before his clothes again became infected, and then, in obedience to instructions, he should once more seek entrance No. 1 and again go through the cleansing process. This would have provided the whole Battery with harmless amusement throughout the day, but fortunately there were only fifteen spare suits at each section, so the war was won after all!

During the night March 3rd/4th, the Hun subjected Bailleul and the Forward Section to a heavy bombardment of gas and H.E. There were concentrations from 10.2 p.m. to 10.55 p.m., from 3.2 a.m. to 4.28 a.m., and again from 5.10 a.m. to 5.34 a.m. In all, the enemy must have fired about 1,100 rounds. While the shelling lasted things were anything but pleasant, but fortunately there was not a single casualty.

The next day the Major (in compliance with the instructions received at the conference on the 2nd) had to leave the Forward Section and join the Main Section at "X2." Lieutenant S. R. Wood took over command of the forward guns. Lieutenant Jones was with him, and the same day Lieutenant Minns was sent up from the Rear Section, it being necessary to keep at least three officers forward.

On March 5th Lieutenant Hill arrived at Aubigny from Calais with six 8-inch Mark VII howitzers which were to replace the Mark VI's with which the Battery was armed. The same day, the late gas concentration at the Forward Section began to cause some casualties. Seven men went to hospital, including Corporal Mauchlin, who had been with the Battery since its very early days. He was a great loss. The next day there were eight more gas casualties from the position at "S"; all of them went to hospital, and only one ever rejoined the Battery. In the afternoon three more "young officers" made their appearance, among them being Second Lieutenant E. J. Noakes, who was afterwards posted to the Battery.

On March 7th the Battery suffered another loss. Lieutenant S. R. Wood, who had stuck it bravely at the Forward Section, became a gas casualty. He had been with the Battery since its formation, and enjoyed the entire confidence of both officers and men. He was evacuated, and, although he never returned to the Battery, he was often remembered and always with pleasure. This was not the only misfortune: Lieutenant Minns, who had done very useful work during the four months he had been with the Battery, was also gassed and forced to go sick, together with four other ranks. Lieutenant Allen went "Forward" to replace Lieutenant Wood. Second Lieutenant Jones was the only officer with him, and there were only three at the rear position; this, too, was at a time when there was heavy work on hand.

About this time the Corps H.A. realised that the Battery's guns at the rear position were unduly cramped with the 9·2-inch howitzers of 69 Siege Battery, and instructions came through that we were to move our guns to a position south of the Bailleul Road. This came as a sad blow to the Battery, as we had put in a lot of work at the "X2" position in constructing two mined dug-outs, numerous cartridge recesses and some good pits. All these would, of course, be taken over by "69." Major Heath made a strong protest to the Brigade Commander, and the injustice which would result was so obvious that the instructions were cancelled and the 9·2's were ordered to move instead. Of course it was unfortunate for them, but doubtless they saw the fairness of the arrangement, and in order to help to lessen their task, Major Heath lent them a party of men to assist in the move. A few days later an exchange of billets took place, 69 Siege taking over those of ours in the railway cutting which were quite near to their new position, and we occupying, in exchange, those in the "X2" position which had formerly been used by the 9·2-inch battery. Major Heath, with prophetic foresight, saw that, in the event of a Hun attack, the railway cutting would come in for a good deal of attention, and consequently he rather welcomed the new arrangement.

On the night of March 10th/11th the Mark VI howitzers at "S" position were pulled out and replaced by Mark VII's, and the next night a similar exchange as regards two guns took place at the rear position. The next day the first shoot with the new guns was done from the "S" position, with an aeroplane ranging. After fourteen rounds had been fired the screen of camouflage in front of No. 2 gun took fire and burned so fiercely that all the men had to be taken off the gun to put it out. It was found impossible to extinguish the blaze, so the Major (who had gone to the forward position to witness the shoot) put the gun out of action and continued ranging with the other gun which was still concealed from the Hun. The enemy's O.P. work seems to have been very poor, for the burning screen and the men working to put it out must have been plainly visible from his lines. It is possible, however, that he may have considered it inadvisable to destroy the position, having in mind the likelihood of the Section pulling out and going elsewhere, and the possible lapse of a fortnight or so before the new position could be discovered with accuracy. If he had any intention of attacking in the near future, it would obviously be to his advantage to keep our batteries in their known positions, which would certainly help him to neutralise, and possibly destroy them immediately he attacked.

The same night two more 8-inch Mark VII's arrived at the rear position to replace the two remaining Mark VI's. An unfortunate thing happened. Lieutenant Hill was in charge of the job, and before getting the last gun in, he took Lieutenant Smythe, the A.S.C. officer who had brought the guns up, to show him the pit and the various obstacles he would have to clear. While they were together the enemy put over a burst of 4.2's, which fell just round the pit. Lieutenant Smythe was killed outright and Lieutenant Hill had one leg blown off. Lieutenant Smythe was an officer belonging to the column of one of the other batteries in the Brigade, and at the time that he was so unfortunately killed, was deputising for Lieutenant Beavan, A.S.C., who, for some reason, was prevented from superintending the move. Lieutenant Hill was a great loss to us; he was a very steady and efficient officer and was liked by all.

The forward position at "S" continued to have the worst of times; and the vicinity was shelled at intervals during both day and night; the enemy using a large number of gas shells. On the 12th, there were fourteen casualties, wounded or gassed; one, Gunner Lynch—a thoroughly good fellow—dying of his wounds. The next day eight more casualties were reported from the position, and it was arranged that detachments off duty should retire to "N" position, where work, as has already been mentioned, had been abandoned. As a further precaution, Brigade ordered that the personnel at "S," when not in gas-proof dug-outs, should wear box respirators. This instruction was carried out as far as possible, but it was hardly practicable for gas masks to be constantly worn in view of the immense amount of work to be done in the position. Besides the heavy programme of firing, ammunition had to be unloaded from the Decauville by

BAILLEUL CHURCH.
(About Fifty Yards North of "S." Position.)

night and taken about 200 yards to the guns. The camouflage screen in front of the guns had constantly to be repaired, and the work of keeping the position in anything like order after its daily strafing from the Hun, was enormous. It was a physical impossibility for the men to carry out all these duties day after day hampered with box respirators. In fairness it must be said that the Staff at Corps realised the difficulties which had to be met. General East, the G.O.C., H.A., showed his sympathy in a practical way by sending his groom up to the position to assist in ammunition fatigues.

On March 14th Gunner Williams, another good man, was unfortunately killed while going down to the water-point, and four more casualties from gas were suffered at "S." These were Sergeant Hansell, Corporal (acting Sergeant) Slinger, Bombardier Medley and Gunner Cross. Sergeant Hansell had come to France with the Battery, and had several acts of bravery to his credit, for which the Major had sought, unavailingly, to get him rewarded. Fortunately none of these were badly gassed, but they were all evacuated and thus lost to the Battery. Sergeant Slinger had done splendid work. For some time he had been acting as B.C.A. at "S," and had proved himself so thoroughly efficient and fearless that it was difficult to imagine how he could be replaced. Bombardier McKenzie was put in his place, and his selection was fully justified by the splendid way in which he carried on.

The next two days further enemy gas-shelling was suffered at "S," while "X2" came in for a certain amount of attention from a 4·2-inch howitzer, which destroyed some ammunition. On the 17th there was another casualty at "S," and on the day following, Lieutenant W. R. Jones was obliged to go sick from the effects of gas. He had been at the forward position since February 1st, and had stuck it well. He was evacuated for the time being, but the Battery was able to welcome him back some two months later.

Lieutenant Allen was thus left alone at "S" until Second Lieutenant Curtis was sent from "X2" to help him. This left the Major with only two officers at the rear position.

Just about this time the Corps promoted a competition among the batteries as to which could exhibit (1) the best covered pit, (2) the best open pit. The prizes were to be a special leave to England for the No. 1 and one other of the successful detachment. On the morning of the 18th, Generals Mercer, G.O.C., R.A., and East, G.O.C., H.A., and Colonel Curteis, commanding the 83rd Brigade, visited the Battery to adjudicate. Most of the pits were in course of being changed from open to covered pits, but it was thought that there was a sporting chance for Sergeant Irvine's. It had been dressed up very well in spite of the fact that the slit trench and one cartridge recess had been blown in by the inconsiderate Hun too recently to allow time for the necessary repair. There was great jubilation when it was adjudged by the Generals to be the second best in the Corps, and one special leave was granted as a second prize. The first prize was carried off by a battery situated farther north, in a much quieter and more peaceful locality which allowed rather more leisure for the application of the " spit and polish " process. There were amusing episodes when Commanders of other batteries presented themselves at the position under orders from the General, to inspect Sergeant Irvine's pit as one which they should endeavour to imitate. It was difficult for the Battery to hide its blushes on such occasions, and it is said (though not corroborated) that the Major was wont to welcome such visitors in his gas mask.

March 21st will for long be remembered as the day on which the German attack was launched against the Fifth Army opposite Amiens. On the same day, at 5 a.m., the Hun commenced bombarding the Battery. In spite of this, between 4 a.m. and 7.37 a.m., the Rear Section fired 116 rounds on various " Programme Targets," working most of the time in gas masks. After the enemy bombardment had ceased (7.30 a.m.), a party under Bombardier Allen (the Gas N.C.O.) were told off to strew all recent shell holes with chloride of lime. Spare charges were also burnt in these holes to disperse the gas ; but in spite of all these precautions there were five gas casualties the next day.

On March 22nd orders came through from H.Q. instructing us to get all guns on to their emergency platforms. These were plank platforms which had been put down near the pits, and from which the guns would have a greatly extended zone of fire. This was done, and we were thus enabled on the next day, when the Hun attacked south of the Scarpe, to give all the help possible.

Monchy-le-Preux fell to the Hun, and this made an attack on the Battery's front almost certain. The same day orders came through to evacuate the position at "S," and to bring the two guns over from the forward side of the Vimy Ridge to a position in rear, where there were two pits which had been prepared by some other battery but never occupied. This move was carried out by Lieutenants Allen and Curtis, and the guns were in action in their new position on the morning of the 24th. The Vickers platforms and ammunition were left at "S" to be fetched later, as no transport was available. There was not a single tear shed at leaving the position where so many good fellows had been either wounded or killed, and the survivors had good reason to consider themselves lucky.

There was now unmistakable evidence of the impending enemy attack on our immediate front. The Hun began moving his artillery up, and the number of his pieces was being increased daily. He was not, however, allowed to do this with impunity, as the following note from Major Heath's diary will show:

"About noon (March 23rd) the Brigade Commander rang up and informed me that the Field Artillery had spotted a battery of 5·9-inch howitzers in the open and asked us to fire with their observation. I got into communication with the R.F.A., and finding that their O.P. was not far away, decided to go up and range the guns myself. Their Brigade Commander pointed out to me the target—four black objects which could just be seen on the plain south of Neuvireuil (C. 14D, 6-6). I opened fire, but the light became so bad that it was impossible to observe. The Field gunners promised to ring me up should the light improve. I returned to the Battery as there was plenty of work to be done there. At about 4.30 the Field gunners rang up to announce with great joy that they could see the four guns again quite plainly. I made for the O.P. at once and found that four howitzers, in line, could be plainly seen. We opened fire and had a splendid shoot. At the time I could only be certain that one gun was directly 'O.K.'d.' We also caused three large dumps to go up, and three smaller flares, evidently cartridges. The next morning I had occasion to go up to the front line near Oppy Wood, and found on closer

"X2" POSITION.

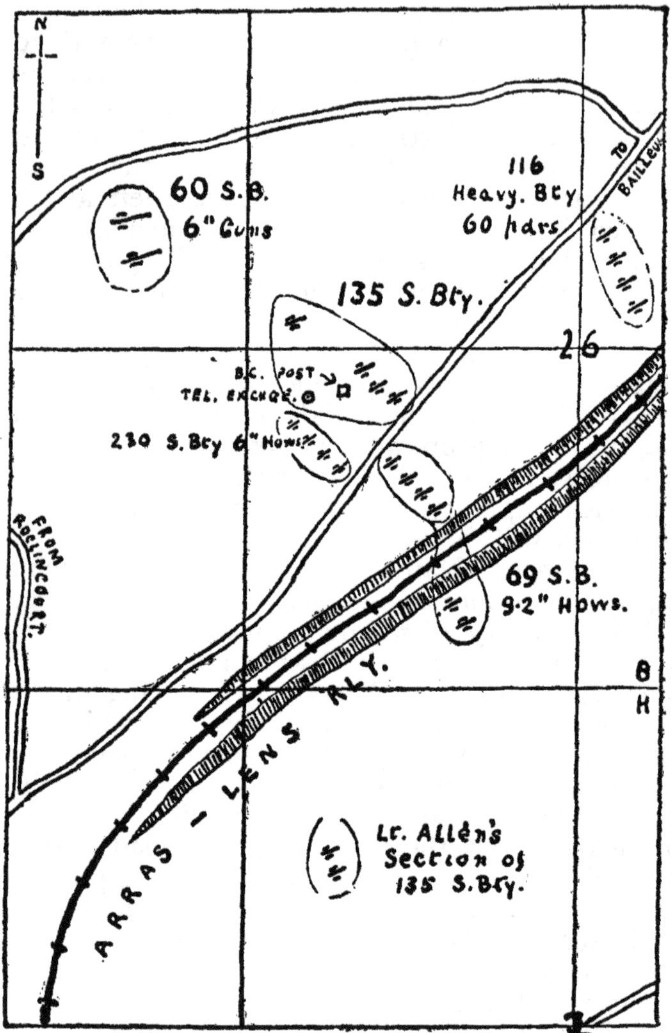

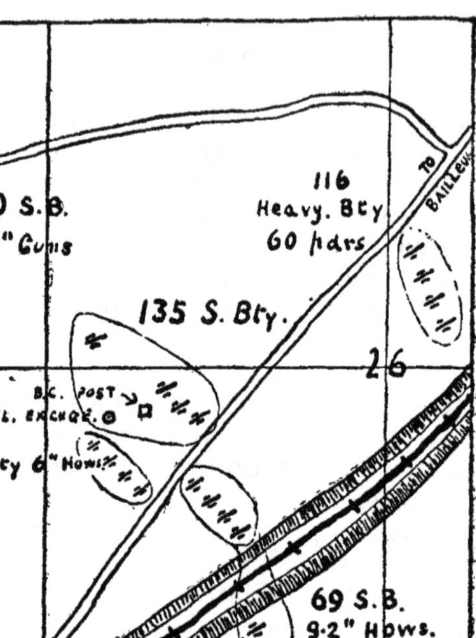

Scale $\frac{1}{10,000}$. Sides of Squares 500 yds.

examination, in a good light, that Nos. 2, 3 and 4 were certainly destroyed, and that No. 1, although still distinguishable, was certainly damaged."

On the 25th there were three casualties from gas at "X2": Sergeant Darby, Gunner Gellatly and Corporal Harding, the last named being the No. 1 of No. 1 gun. All these returned to the Battery about two months later. On the morning of the next day the Hun began shelling about 200 yards short of the Battery. Only one round landed actually inside the Battery, and that unfortunately wounded Gunner Herbert. He was badly hurt in the head and died about a month later. He was a very good fellow and was greatly missed by his detachment.

The disposition of the two Sections of the Battery and its relative position to other batteries in the Brigade on the morning of March 27th is shown in the accompanying diagram. This day was the quietest that the Battery had experienced for a long time—a fact in itself portentous. Advantage was taken of this and all the guns at "X2" were registered at second charge. Night fell on a very quiet front. Lieutenants Hooper and Noakes were on duty in the B.C. post. Midnight found everything still peaceful, but the 28th was not to be allowed to dawn in such calm. At 3.15 a.m. precisely, the storm burst with a violent enemy bombardment on the right. At 3.30 a.m. the Battery was heavily shelled with gas. Every one was roused and the usual gas precautions taken. As yet no firing orders had come through from Brigade, and the Major gave instructions for all men not actually required on the guns to clear out of the gassed area. Lieutenants T. R. Wood and O. L. Gill (the latter an officer who had joined the Battery on the 26th) were detailed to go with them and to keep the men together so as to be ready to supply reliefs. At 4 a.m. S.O.S. was ordered by Brigade, and this order was repeated at 5.36 a.m. About 6 a.m. the gas shelling ceased, but a very heavy H.E. fire continued. It was chiefly from 4·2-inch and 5·9-inch howitzers, but on No. 4 gun (Sergeant Baldwin) there was an 8-inch, or possibly an 11-inch, which was making itself most objectionable. Rounds were falling very close, both plus and minus of the gun. In addition, all the other batteries in the Brigade were being heavily shelled, and the central position occupied by us accounted for a large number of rounds being received which were probably intended for other of the batteries. At 6.20 a.m., "Counter General" was ordered, and forty-five rounds fired, chiefly by Nos. 3 and 4 guns. At 8 a.m., the fire on the position being very heavy, the detachments of Nos. 1 and 2 guns were put under cover in the deep dug-out. At 8.14 a.m. No. 4 gun was reported "out of action." Fire was ordered on Oppy Wood, and this was carried out by No. 3 gun (Sergeant Lockley). No. 4 had its trail absolutely buried. One shell had landed just in rear of the pit, and another had broken the right wheel and blown in the slit-trench cartridge recess. The trail was dug out, but it was found impossible to traverse the gun. The dial sight was also damaged. Major Heath put Lieutenant Hooper in charge and ordered the gun to be fired at the line it was then on, with slight variations in the elevation.

About midday the enemy fire slackened, but increased again about 2.20 p.m. At 2.22 p.m. Brigade ordered fire to be opened on the road south of Oppy Wood and to be continued regardless of casualties. Thereupon all guns were immediately put into action. Lieutenant T. R. Wood had charge of No. 3, and Lieutenant Gill took charge of Nos. 1 and 2. Lieutenant Gill showed great coolness and courage, which was especially praiseworthy as he had only been with the Battery a few days.

The shelling continued until 5.30 p.m., but in spite of this, officers and men stuck to the guns, which continued firing. From 2.30 p.m. to 6.30 p.m. 221 rounds were fired from "X2" position, which was quite a creditable performance considering the delay caused by the damaged condition of the pits. Most of the cartridge recesses had been hit, and some were burning for a considerable time.

At 7 p.m. General East, G.O.C., H.A., visited the position and spoke to the men. He showed his appreciation of their work by helping to roll some shells up to the guns.

The casualties during the day were surprisingly slight. Bombardier (acting Corporal) J. E. Jackson from No. 1 gun and Gunner Townsend both died later of wounds received, and there were nine others wounded, which included Gunners Dove, Child, Clough, Iliffe, Hill, T., Styles, Morton, Chapman and Acting Bombardier Collyer. The two last named were gassed and went to hospital some days later.

One gun (No. 4) was put out of action and its platform was badly damaged. No. 1 gun was fortunate to have been on its emergency plank platform, as the Vickers platform in the pit out of which the gun had been drawn was completely destroyed by several hits. A large number of smaller stores were also burnt or damaged.

A few words must be said in praise of Lieutenant Allen's Section, which did very useful work during the battle. The position had only been occupied four days before, and consequently had not been located by the enemy. It came in for an unpleasant amount of shelling, especially from an 8-inch, but generally did not get punished in the same way as the older position. Lieutenant Curtis, who was with Lieutenant Allen, seems to have done some useful dribbling with a hand-cart in search of a further supply of cartridges. It was afterwards discovered that he was a useful rugger man. On this occasion he converted an excellent "try," as he actually returned with some cartridges.

No. 3 gun, under Sergeant Lockley, acquitted itself well in remaining in action nearly all day. There was fairly good cover to the pit, but courage and steadiness also played an important part. Bombardier Lancaster did good work on No. 2 gun in keeping up a steady rate of fire during the afternoon under heavy bombardment. The cartridge recess near the gun was blown in and blazed for a long time: Gunner W. Jones, the cartridge number, worked hard and bravely in feeding the gun from a more distant recess. Sergeant Baldwin and his detachment on the damaged No. 4 gun also did good work during the afternoon.

Great credit is due to the Battery signallers, inasmuch as telephonic communication was maintained with Brigade throughout the battle. With one exception, all other batteries in the Brigade had their lines cut beyond repair, and we were consequently made use of by Headquarters in delivering communications to other batteries. Gunner H. Brookes did excellent work in carrying these messages under heavy fire. Bombardier Wickenden and his party of linesmen must also be mentioned for their steadiness in repairing the frequently cut wires between the Telephone Exchange and the B.C. Post.

Doubtless there were many others who were also responsible for courageous acts. The fact that they are not mentioned here does not mean that they did not further the good cause, but a complete list of "mentions" would probably include most of the personnel of the Battery.

It was Lieutenant Stevens who, unconsciously, supplied the "funny turn" of the day. He was rejoining the Battery from overseas leave, and during his short fortnight seems to have contrived to forget all about the war. At any rate, during the heavy shelling he sauntered into the Battery in slacks, with swagger cane, suitcase and soft cap complete. A straw hat would have looked much more in keeping, but that must have been in the suitcase with his dress clothes!

So ended the great attack of March 28th. We fear that it has been dealt with here inadequately, but during such a strenuous day diaries have to be neglected. It may be of interest to include the official account which was circulated by Corps a few days later. It will be noticed that, although the work of the Battery is not specially referred to, the 83rd Brigade generally is accorded no small measure of praise.

NARRATIVE OF ARTILLERY OPERATIONS IN CONNECTION WITH GERMAN ATTACK ON GAVRELLE—OPPY SECTOR, MARCH 28TH, 1918.

On the morning of the attack the 56th Division was holding a line from South of Gavrelle to Arleux, a front of about 5,000 yards.

Artillery Available.

To cover this front the artillery available was:—

R.F.A.

56th Divisional Artillery and nine guns of 52nd Army Brigade R.F.A., i.e., forty-five 18-pounders and twelve 4.5-inch howitzers.

R.G.A.

83rd Brigade R.G.A. consisting of:

Ten - - - -	60-pounders.
Six - - - -	9·2-inch howitzers.
Six - - - -	8-inch howitzers.
Eleven - - - -	6-inch howitzers.
Two - - - -	6-inch Mark VII Guns.

In addition, the 16th Brigade R.G.A. consisting of two 60-pounder Batteries and two 6-inch Howitzer Batteries was available to assist with Counter-Battery work.

None of the guns of the 1st and 3rd Canadian Brigades R.G.A., which were temporarily attached to XIII Corps, were able to give direct assistance to the front attacked.

Signs of Attack.

Between 3.0 a.m. and 3.30 a.m. a hostile barrage consisting of both gas shell and H.E. of all calibres was put down on the support and red lines.

At 4.0 a.m. the barrage increased over the whole front system and the "Posts" were heavily bombarded by T.M.'s. This continued until 7.15 a.m.

Counter Preparation.

During the above periods, i.e., from 3.0 a.m. to 7.15 a.m., our artillery was firing heavily on the enemy's front system of trenches, special concentrations being put down by R.F.A. and H.A. in co-operation, on lines of organised shell holes. It was considered at the time that these shell holes were temporary trench mortar emplacements, but from information given by prisoners after the attack it appears likely that they were the assembly positions of assaulting troops.

At 6.45 a.m. counter preparation was put into effect. This consisted of a barrage of Field and Heavy Artillery on enemy's likely forming-up places searching backwards and forwards.

At 7.15 a.m. the hostile barrage lifted from our front line to the support line, and the S.O.S. went up in the Gavrelle sector and was repeated almost immediately in the Oppy sector.

Barrage.

From this time until about 11.0 a.m., mixed fighting was taking place in our front line system. Artillery Group Commanders adjusted their barrage lines as required in consultation with Infantry Brigade Commanders concerned.

At 11.0 a.m., a withdrawal to the Bailleul—Willerval (Red Line) having been previously ordered, a protective barrage was put down by Field and Heavy Artillery in front of this line (assistance being given by nine 18-pounders of the 3rd Canadian Divisional Artillery on the left).

Targets in the Open.

From 11.0 a.m. till about 3.0 p.m. many excellent targets in the open were engaged by both Field and Heavy Artillery with great effect. One notable performance was that of 284th Siege Battery, who got direct hits on three of four enemy guns firing in the open from South of Oppy Wood, and blew up most of their ammunition. Bodies of troops and transport was freely engaged with direct observation.

Unfortunately, owing to the limited number of guns available to cover the front, only a few could be taken off the barrage at a time to deal with these targets.

Masses of hostile infantry, transport and batteries in the open were visible in all directions.

Afternoon Attack on Red Line.

At about 3.30 p.m. the enemy made a heavy attack against the Red Line, particularly on Bailleul East Post.

This was completely shattered by a concentrated barrage of Heavy and Field Artillery, Rifle and Machine-gun fire.

Hostile Barrage on Our Battery Positions.

At 3.15 a.m. a heavy gas shell and H.E. bombardment was opened on our Battery positions. No gas was used after 6 a.m.

The bombardment of Battery positions continued at an intense rate until about 12 noon, when it slackened considerably, but was maintained throughout the day until about 5 p.m., when the enemy's last attack on the Red Line failed. The bombardment was from several batteries and included 21cm., 5·9-inch and 4·2-inch howitzers, and 5·9-inch and 4·2-inch guns (H.V.) Possibly one 20cm. howitzer was also firing.

The gas was fired by 77 mm. guns.

The shelling was more in the nature of area shoots than definite Counter-Battery fire.

Battery Positions which Escaped Hostile Barrage.

Two days prior to the attack, eight Heavy Artillery pieces forward of the Ridge were withdrawn and put into action in new positions on the Ridge. These guns escaped the hostile barrage altogether.

The H.A. Batteries on the Bailleul road suffered most from the hostile barrage.

Advanced Arleux Valley Section.

A section of the 93rd Battery (18-pounders) in position as an enfilade section near Arleux in front of the Red Line, engaged many targets with observation from the vicinity of the guns and was fought till our Infantry withdrew through it. The detachments then retired, on orders, after damaging the guns, burning the dugouts and removing dial sights and breech blocks.

Damage to Equipment.

Field Artillery.—Twelve 18-pounders were destroyed or put out of action by enemy shell fire, and the two 18-pounders in the Arleux Valley had to be destroyed.

Heavy Artillery.—Guns continued to go out of action from enemy shell fire, but only three 60-pounders and one 8-inch howitzer were permanently crippled.

Many guns and howitzers of the H.A. had been pulled out of their pits prior to the attack in order to get sufficient switch to assist the XVII Corps. This made them more vulnerable to splinters of hostile shells. During the day some of the lighter natures were got back into their pits in the intervals of firing. Many temporary disablements occurred owing to guns being partially buried by explosion of shell and the fittings having to be replaced.

Casualties.

	Officers.			Other Ranks.		
	Killed.	Wounded.	Missing.	Killed.	Wounded.	Missing.
R.F.A. - -	–	3	1	11	29	8
R.G.A. - -	3	5	–	11	69	–
Total R.A. Casualties -	3	8	1	22	98	8

Ammunition Expenditure.

R.F.A.—From early 28th till 29th March—expenditure of ammunition was about 23,000 rounds 18-pounder and 8,000 rounds of 4·5-inch howitzers. This does not include the expenditure of the nine 18-pounders of the 52nd Army Brigade.

Since during a part of the 28th March a number of guns up to fourteen were permanently out of action, the expenditure resulting would appear to be about:

750 rounds per 18-pounder.
650 rounds per 4·5-inch howitzer.

R.G.A.—83rd Brigade R.G.A.

116th Heavy Battery - - - - - -	1,975	
1/1 Highland Heavy Battery - - -	561	(One Section knocked out.)
60th Siege Battery (6-inch Mk. VII.) - -	258	
69th Siege Battery (9·2-inch howitzer) - -	700	
135th Siege Battery (8-inch howitzer) - -	797	
230th Siege Battery (6-inch howitzer) - -	1,658	
284th Siege Battery (6-inch howitzer) - -	2,460	

Withdrawal of Batteries.

During the night 28/29th March, all Divisional Artillery with the exception of two batteries was withdrawn to positions at average range of about 3,600 yards to our new front line. This move was carried out by single guns of Batteries in turn. Harassing fire was maintained throughout the night.

On night 28/29th March, the 83rd Brigade R.G.A. began the withdrawal of Batteries on the Bailleul road. This was completed successfully the following night.

Trench Mortars.

All the six 8-inch T.M.'s in the front line system were lost to the enemy and no news is obtainable as to the fate of the officer and detachments of the two which were manned.

The three 6-inch T.M.'s covering the Red Line later in the day fired on various occasions at the request of the Infantry and in answer to the S.O.S. signals.

Communications.

Communications to some of the O.P.'s were cut, but on the whole they were well and bravely maintained. These wires were in most cases not buried. Where wires had been properly buried they stood.

Communications from Groups to Batteries were maintained throughout. These wires had been recently buried.

In one case an officer was observing from a point 200 yards from the bury to which an overland cable had been laid. This was repeatedly cut by shell fire and found impossible to maintain. On moving back to a test point on the bury, he was able to get equally good observation, and kept through by telephone the whole time.

Visual (Lucas Lamp) Signalling was resorted to on one or two occasions and, though slow, proved its value.

C.W. Wireless kept through in one case from Brigade to a Forward Battery, when all other means failed. The ærial was shot down and re-erected many times.

Pigeons were used from certain O.P.'s with success. If lofts are situated at Corps or Brigade Headquarters, this is undoubtedly a valuable means of communication, but if information has to be transmitted by telephone the information usually arrives too late.

General.

The fire of the Batteries of the 83rd Brigade R.G.A. appears to have been accurate and effective. Possibly this was largely due to their being well registered with the lowest possible charge at the shortest possible range prior to, and in anticipation of, the attack. On our withdrawal to the Red Line this proved of the greatest value.

Heavy shell with 106 Fuze as usual proved their exceptional value against troops in the open.

Our Counter-Battery Action.

Harassing fire was carried out during the night previous to the attack, and this may account for hostile Batteries being brought into action after the attack was launched.

The 83rd Brigade R.G.A. was engaged on counter programmes during the night previous to the attack and was not available for C.B. work. It was therefore difficult to keep down the fire of the Batteries in the south of our area.

The 12-inch and 6-inch Mk. XIX Guns of 26th H.A.G. however were employed for this purpose.

At 11 a.m. the G.O.C. 56th Division asked for C.B. work on account of the heavy shelling of the Point Du Jour, and from then on, 83rd Brigade R.G.A. was employed on C.B. work.

Visibility from the ridge was very good, and the neutralisation was reported to be effective: several explosions were seen. The areas in which forward Batteries were located were kept under fire all day, and a concentration of three Brigades was fired on a " nest " of Batteries in Fresnoy Park.

It did not appear that there had been any large increase in the strength of the hostile artillery as estimated previously, but all had moved forward.

Enemy's batteries dribbled into action and were in unprotected positions. They presented vulnerable targets. If more guns had been available for C.B. work from the start more execution might have been done.

Hostile batteries did not disclose themselves until the opening of the bombardment, and avoided all positions previously active.

CONCLUSION

The following points are worthy of notice :—

1. *Replacement of Guns and Personnel of Heavy and Siege Batteries.*

A severe strain was put on the personnel of the Heavy and Siege Batteries, especially on the 83rd Brigade R.G.A. Harassing fire had been kept up during the previous night. On the day of the attack most of the batteries were heavily shelled. The mere physical labour of handling the heavy shell—100 to 200 lbs. in weight—was great. Casualties were heavy. Fire had to be kept up all day.

In a defensive battle, when the enemy develops heavy counter-battery fire, this severe strain on all batteries within range of hostile heavy howitzers is sure to occur. If batteries are to remain in action under heavy fire for over twenty-four hours, an increase in the personnel is essential, and the casualties must be replaced without delay. To meet this, the following suggestions are made :—

(*a*) A pool of guns and personnel to be always held by the Army by keeping out of the line a Mixed Brigade R.G.A. and using this Brigade as a pool.

(*b*) Utilising the personnel of any super-howitzers which go out of action, in order to help Heavy and Siege Batteries in the line.

2. *Replacement of 18-pounders and 4-5-inch Howitzers.*

When the front held by a Division is extensive, and that front is covered by one Divisional Artillery only, it is essential that 18-pounders and 4·5-inch howitzers, which are knocked out, should be replaced immediately. In case of a hostile attack this is of vital importance.

In the case in point, twelve of the thirty-six available 18-pounders in the line were knocked out. These had to be replaced by guns brought from Bruay, distant eleven miles by road. This took a considerable time.

It is suggested that a pool of 18-pounders and 4·5-inch howitzers up to 20 per cent. of the number of guns in the line should be kept at the Corps Ordnance Workshops. This pool should be under the control of the Corps, and should be utilized for the immediate replacement of guns and howitzers which have been knocked out or damaged.

3. *Communications.*

(*a*) Lines to O.P.'s where buried, stood throughout the day.

Where not buried, they were cut, and the O.P. was useless until the line had been repaired.

If it is not possible to have a buried line to the O.P. then a series of Relay Posts must be established in each line, one telephonist and one linesman at each Relay Post.

(*b*) Trench warfare has taught us to place so much reliance on the telephone, that the training of orderlies (both mounted and dismounted) has been allowed to lapse to a large extent. The training of runners and orderlies is a most important matter if they are to be of value.

(*c*) When Corps Headquarters moved to Acq, communication between the Corps R.A. and the Heavy and Divisional Artillery was very unsatisfactory.

Had there been a hostile attack along the whole Corps front, it would have been very difficult to co-ordinate artillery fire after the move of Corps H.Q. took place.

4. *Lorries.*

It is dangerous to take ammunition lorries for transport of Infantry, when an engagement is possible. The Heavy Artillery started the fight with over 100 lorries short.

5. *Direct Observation.*

Many excellent targets in the open presented themselves, and were successfully engaged by both Heavy and Field Artillery with direct observation.

The 56th Divisional Artillery, however, report that "owing to the limited number of guns available to cover the front, only a few could be taken off the barrage at one time to deal with the targets."

The value of a barrage, such as we have become accustomed to in trench warfare, is very small compared with the value of the fire of a battery on to an hostile body of troops, which can be seen and taken on with direct observation. In my opinion, the proper procedure in such a case would be, that barrage fire should be suspended, and that each Battery should devote its whole attention to engaging targets with direct observation. Each Battery should be allotted a zone or " lane " for this purpose.

About 8 p.m. on the 28th orders came through that we were to retire that night to Ecurie railway station, and to make full use of the plank railroad so as to be in action before daylight in the event of the enemy continuing his attack. Fortunately the shelling had ceased, and throughout the night there were only occasional bursts, so that we were able to pull out without much trouble. After several unsuccessful attempts to get the damaged (No. 4) gun on to the road, we decided to leave it behind for the time being. The wheel was knocked out of shape and some of the spokes were missing, so that delay, only, was likely to result from further attempts to get it away.

We left " X2 " about 3 a.m. and arrived at Ecurie just before 6 a.m. We started firing at 12.45 p.m. on the 29th and continued throughout the afternoon and night until 8 a.m. on the 30th, expending altogether 240 rounds of ammunition.

The platforms were primitive and gave some trouble, as we were so far distant from the Hun lines that all of the firing had to be done at full charge. On the afternoon of the 30th the guns were registered on the willows south of Oppy Wood, Lieutenant Noakes observing from " Edgar " O.P. On his way back, Lieutenant Noakes met a party with Lieutenant Beavan, A.S.C., and the damaged gun was pulled out of the old " X2 " position and taken to an Ordnance workshop for repair. The same night Lieutenant Allen's two guns, which had remained forward, joined us at Ecurie, and pulled in on the right of the other three guns.

Our stay at Ecurie Station was uneventful. The enemy had not thought it advisable to make a further attack, and so, on the afternoon of March 31st, we received orders to move up to a position just north of Ecurie village.*

---

* A. 22c, 7.8.

"SUMMER" O.P.

From a Water Colour Drawing by Lieutenant C. R. Hurle Hobbs.

CHAPTER VIII

Ecurie and Roclincourt

[April—July, 1918]

On the morning of April 1st the five guns were in action in the new position. This was in a camp of Nissen huts, known as Springfield Camp, which occupied a slight hollow west of the Arras—Lens road. On our arrival the huts were in the occupation of a Tank Battalion, who seemed anything but pleased to see five 8-inch howitzers appear on the scene. We were consequently received somewhat coldly. A few days later, and after the guns had been in action during most nights, our friends decided that a quieter spot would be more advantageous to their health, and accordingly they left us in possession of the camp without so much as expressing sorrow at being thus compelled to leave us.

The position was not under direct observation from the enemy, but the ruins of Monchy (by this time once more in the possession of the Hun) could be seen from a point about 100 yards in rear of the guns, so that our flashes were probably visible to the enemy.

We established a new Battery O.P. on the southern end of the Vimy Ridge. This O.P., which was known as "Summer," afforded excellent facilities for observation, and was extremely comfortable. It was splinter proof, and was connected on the left with the entrance to a deep dug-out which had originally been constructed by the Bosche, and was capable of withstanding anything up to an 8-inch shell. It became the practice of the O.C. to have one of the Battery officers continuously at this O.P., and a tour of duty (lasting generally for a fortnight) was undertaken, in turn, by each officer. A bed was fitted up in the deep dug-out, and with valise and blankets very comfortable nights were assured, always providing, of course, that the Bosche behaved himself and remained quiet. Rations were sent up from the Battery daily.

On April 11th one half of the Battery, under Lieutenant Hooper, moved into a forward position, which had been prepared just west of the Roclincourt—Thelus road. It became known as the Plank road position, as it was just south of a road constructed of planks which connected the Arras—Lens road with the Roclincourt—Thelus road. The guns were in good emplacements dug into a bank, while about 100 yards in rear there was a deep dug-out which provided an excellent place for a B.C. Post.

During the early part of April some very unpleasant excursions had to be made to the old positions for the purpose of salving certain stores and material which had been left behind at the time of our hurried departure. At the old "S" position, a Vickers platform and a quantity of ammunition had to be collected, and the work, which could only be done at night, was generally carried out under shell fire of a more or less heavy nature. Lieutenant Gill, who was in charge of these salvage parties, and the men who went with him deserve special mention for the way in which they carried out their difficult job.

In comparison with the strenuous period at "S" and "X2," we had a quiet time throughout the whole of April. The new positions were, as yet, undiscovered by the enemy, and this afforded us time to recover from our recent mauling, and get ourselves ready for the next occasion when the Hun should decide to try again. Although it was not fully appreciated at the time, it is now recognised that had the German attack on the Vimy Ridge been successful, the subsequent course of the war might have been very different. The attacks he had launched in other sectors since the opening of his offensive on March 21st had met with success, and the capture of the Vimy Ridge would have enabled him to exploit these victories to far greater advantage than he was able with the possession of this valuable feature denied to him. The Battery will always feel proud in having taken part in defending the Ridge.

The question which at this time was uppermost in the mind of everyone was as to when the next blow would fall. It was expected daily, and on more than one occasion warning came through from H.Q. that a further enemy attack was to be made on such and such a day.

Everyone, however, was confident that, whenever made, it would be met successfully in spite of the somewhat discouraging news that occasionally reached the Battery of reverses in other sectors.

The Rear Section continued very quiet and did little firing, but the Forward Section, near the Plank road, became very busy towards the end of April, and carried out aeroplane shoots daily. Every night they were responsible for a heavy programme of harassing fire which, from the reports of Hun prisoners, the enemy evidently found extremely unpleasant. This constant firing meant very hard work for the men: the weather was wet, and the three guns which were on plank platforms did their best to go out of action at the slightest provocation. One, No. 450, gave a lot of trouble, and on occasions performed some marvellous acrobatic feats. It developed a propensity for running forward from its scotches on its muzzle, and would keep the men busy in their efforts to right it. During such an operation the attitude of the gun, with its trail high up in the air, was anything but dignified, and the language of the detachment scarcely helped to redeem the situation.

On April 27th, Second Lieutenant C. R. H. Hobbs joined the Battery, and was sent to the forward position. The personnel at this date was distributed as follows :—

Rear Position :

The O.C.
Lieutenants Allen, Curtis, Wood and Gill.
A, B and C Sub-Sections.

Forward Position :

Captain Phillips.
Lieutenants Hooper, Stevens, Noakes and Hobbs.
D, E and F Sub-Sections.

Things remained fairly quiet at the beginning of May, but it was scarcely to be expected that the Forward Section, with its guns so active, could long remain undiscovered. The enemy seems to have found it about May 12th, and at once began to make things rather unpleasant. He made no attempt at a destructive shoot, but contented himself with putting over bursts of harassing fire which, at times, were rather disturbing. On May 17th a round landed only a yard from the trail of No. 1 gun. Fortunately the detachment was under cover at the time, and little damage was done to the gun itself. The next day we were not so fortunate. A round falling in the cookhouse wounded Gunner Douglas rather badly and almost got Sergeant Baldwin. Poor Douglas died on the 20th, and the Battery thus lost a good man and an excellent cook. He had always managed to satisfy the men, and often out of very poor rations. Orderly officers, for weeks after, had good cause to regret him. The same night, about 10.30, a shell penetrated a shack in which three men were sleeping. It was in a trench and had a splinter-proof roof, which must have received most of the force of the explosion, as two of the occupants were practically unhurt. The third, Gunner Taylor, was wounded in the stomach, but behaved so stoically that his injuries were not thought to be serious. He was very much liked in the Battery, and it came as a shock to us when we heard later that he had died in hospital on the 20th.

After May 18th it became apparent that the enemy had decided to subject the Forward Section to some rough treatment, and it was arranged that all officers and men, when off duty, should live at the rear position. A day or two later the Major was instructed by H.Q. to select another position for the forward guns and to clear out of the shelled area as soon as possible.

On May 22nd the enemy made a more determined attempt to destroy the position. Lieutenants Stevens and Hobbs were on B.C. Post duty when an airman called up for a shoot on a prearranged target. It was 4.30 a.m., and it is feared that the energy of the airman in appearing on the scene so early scarcely received the appreciation it merited. The detachments were turned out and the necessary orders having been given to the guns, fire was opened about 4.40 a.m. The shoot promised to be a most successful one, all guns being quickly ranged and an O.K. recorded during the process. The Bosche, however, appears to have been annoyed at being disturbed so early, for it seems that he requisitioned the services of a plane to find out the active battery. Presently he found us, and very soon after commenced shelling the position with a 20-cm. howitzer. It was about 5.30 a.m. when he opened; seventy-two rounds had been fired on the aeroplane target and the observer had gone home. The gun detachments were ordered to seek cover, but whenever the enemy fire slackened they went out and fired a few salvos at the previous elevation. One of the Bosche rounds landed directly on top of the B.C. Post, making a hole about ten feet deep, but the effect inside was nil, with the exception of the sudden extinguishing of every candle. About 6.30, the enemy guns of heavier cabibre became silent, but he continued to bombard the position with 5·9-inch and 4·2-inch shells until well after 9 a.m. Fortunately we had no casualties, but one gun, No. 450, was badly damaged and had to be sent away. Another aeroplane shoot was carried out in the afternoon with the two remaining guns.

The day previous, a new position for the three forward guns had been selected by Major Heath about 800 yards south of the existing position, and 200 yards N.W. of the Roclincourt cross roads. On May 23rd working parties were detailed (chiefly from the rear position) to commence work on the pits. Great care was taken to screen from the enemy's planes all signs of movement in the new position, and camouflage was erected on poles under which the men could work in daylight. The first two pits, when almost complete, had to be abandoned on account of their proximity to the abode of a Brigadier-General. The reason for this can best be explained by recording that it was not the Battery that objected to the Brigadier as a neighbour! New pits were chosen and finished south of the Roclincourt cross roads, and on the night of May 28th, the Forward Half-Battery left the Plank road and occupied these. By daylight all guns were in action. The Major changed places with Captain Phillips and took over the command of the forward guns. Lieutenants Stevens and Noakes went to the rear position and Lieutenant Gill joined Lieutenants Hooper and Hobbs, who both remained forward.

The new position was a picturesque one, amid the ruins of what had once been the village of Roclincourt. There were scarcely two stones remaining intact, but there was plenty of foliage and quite a number of roses which continued to bloom in spite of the Hun. To the left front of No. 1 gun was a large wooden crucifix* which towered majestically above a cluster of trees. It was the only thing left standing in that devastated village. The services of

* A photograph of this appears on the page facing the dedication.

Busty Jackson were requisitioned to repair two old dug-outs which had fallen in. He and his party worked well and ably, and a week or two after our arrival there was, in case of necessity, cover for the whole Section.

On the second day of our occupation of this position, No. 2 gun had a very narrow escape. The enemy put over seven or eight rounds which were probably intended for the cross roads. Four of these fell in the Battery position: one just missed the trail of No. 2 gun by about three yards and buried itself in the cartridge recess. Lieutenant Hobbs and a full detachment were standing round the gun, which was in action at the time, and elevated ready to fire. The whole detachment fell flat and were covered with huge pieces of earth which were thrown up. To Major Heath, who was only about twenty yards off, it seemed that the detachment and its officer had entirely disappeared, but being by nature an optimist, he shouted the order, " No. 2, fire ! " To his surprise he saw the detachment spring to its feet and the No. 2 give a lusty jerk at the lanyard. Why no one was hurt will always remain a mystery. The shell was not by any means a " dud," but must have had a delay-action fuse. Had the fuse been an instantaneous one it is certain that both gun and gunners would have ceased fire for an indefinite period.

It is necessary here to say something about the Rear Half-Battery. Although it had not been so busy as the Forward Section, time had not, by any means, been wasted. The construction of a system of cartridge recesses had been commenced and was completed about the middle of June. "System" is the only word which rightly describes the elaborate scheme of underground passages, with recesses at intervals on either side. Each recess was splinter proof but well ventilated. Surely, they must have been the best in France.

On June 7th one officer and forty-eight other ranks of the Portuguese Heavy Artillery arrived at the rear position. The arrangement was that they should work with the Battery, and thus gain practical experience of the duties of a battery in the field. An N.C.O. and about twenty other ranks were sent to the forward position. On the whole they worked very well. At fatigues, such as shell humping or trench digging, they were excellent, and although for the most part men of small stature, they seemed to be endowed with both strength and endurance. They were

Douai through a telescope from "Summer" O.P.
From a Water Colour Drawing by Lieutenant C. R. Hurle Hobbs.

not used to shell fire and were liable to disappear if shells began falling anywhere within half a mile of the Battery. No doubt they would have got over this in time and have proved very good gunners.

Second Lieutenant Jones, who had been gassed at "S" on March 18th, rejoined the Battery from England about the middle of May. A few weeks later leave, which had been suspended since the commencement of the enemy's spring offensive, was reopened, and allotments began to come through for the Battery.

The beginning of July still found the front comparatively quiet. Both Sections were now carrying out aeroplane shoots daily, and the original ranging sheets had to be sent to Headquarters for the inspection of the Colonel, who never passed without comment anything in the nature of a doubtful correction. We considered ourselves rather good at these shoots, and, as a justification, it may be added here that in the paper published by the XVIIth Corps Heavy Artillery, we figured as second of the three batteries which were mentioned as having done the best counter-battery work with aeroplane observation during the preceding six months.

Towards the end of July a rumour became prevalent that the whole Brigade was going out on rest. The Battery lived in great hopes in spite of a spectre of the last "rest," which seems to have paid nightly visitations to the Major's couch. Our expectations were once more shattered when it became known that the Brigade and four batteries were, in fact, to pull out and go behind the line for a time, but that we and 69 Siege were to join the 67th Brigade R.G.A. and exchange positions with two batteries of the Canadian Heavy Artillery. The great improvements to the existing positions which we had effected recently must have sorely tempted the gods to enforce a move, and the fact that a new officers' mess had been completed at the rear position and was only waiting to be occupied, probably furnished the last straw!

Our stay in the Ecurie and Roclincourt positions, although uneventful, had been rather pleasant. Stationary warfare after a time is liable to become somewhat monotonous, but for the officers, "Summer" O.P. always provided a change of scenery and a bracing tonic. In making this last reference to "Summer," a word of praise must be accorded to those men who, from time to time, acted as the O.P. rationing party. Provisions had to be carried up daily, and the approach along Towy track was never very healthy. It is remarkable that not a single casualty was suffered during the four months that the O.P. was thus served.

On the night of July 22nd the Battery moved into a position just in front of Souchez, the Canadians having taken over from us the positions we were vacating.

CHAPTER IX

Souchez

[July, 1918]

The new position was in the deep valley of the Souchez River and east of the village of Souchez. It had every natural advantage and good flash cover was provided by the high ridge, which rose immediately in front of the position. The guns were distributed over an area of about 800 yards from north to south. Two pits were in each case close together, so that we found ourselves divided into three Sections, Right, Centre and Left. The position was a long way from the German front line, and the enemy being conspicuously weak as regards long-range guns in this sector, our stay promised to be an unusually quiet one.

On the top of the hill in front of us, and only about five minutes distant from the position, was an excellent O.P. know as "Phyllis." The excitement it provided was of a less thrilling nature than we had been accustomed to at "Summer," but it gave a very fair view of the country over which we were to fire and afforded interesting observation on Lens, Sallaumines, Annay and Harnes, while far away in the distance, the Cathedral of Douai could be seen.

The B.C. Post was situated between the Centre and Left Sections and was rather small. There was no dug-out accommodation, which seemed to us to be a disadvantage at first, but we soon appreciated that none was necessary in such a quiet spot. Altogether it was a delightful place, and it is true to say that during our short stay not a single shell fell anywhere near the position. This does not mean that we had nothing to do, for there were several improvements to be carried out before the position could be considered as being in good order. The cartridge recesses were very poor and quite inadequate, and work was commenced at once to provide something better. The detachments worked very well, and when we pulled out, eight days later, we left there several good recesses completed and others in course of construction. There was also a reserve position which had been constructed by the Canadians some months previous and which we found had become flooded, the ammunition being in some cases almost under water. Some hard work was expended in pumping out the water and rebuilding the pits.

An average amount of firing was done and some very successful aeroplane shoots were carried out. Most of the work fell upon the two northern Sections, as the Right Section was a " silent " Section, and only took part in special shoots, such as Corps salvos and concentrations.

On July 28th Lieutenant Hooper went on leave to England. While at home he unfortunately became ill and was not able to rejoin us. Lieutenant Hooper had done excellent work during the time he had been with the Battery, his professional knowledge of structural work being especially useful.

Orders came through on the 29th that we were to pull out of the position the next day and rejoin our own (the 83rd) Brigade at Gouy-Servins. It was rumoured that something in the nature of a big show was to take place shortly, but we had long since learnt to distrust rumours, good or bad, and there seemed nothing particularly exciting in being ordered to rejoin our old Brigade, which we knew to be on " rest."

The guns reported " out of action " at 4 p.m. on July 30th, and as soon as it was dark the move was commenced. The Right and Centre Sections got away in pretty good time, but the Left Section was delayed considerably in the taking up of one of the Vickers platforms. It had been down for some months and was of an early pattern, having been left behind by the Canadian Battery in exchange for one of our platforms which we had left at Roclincourt. It was almost daylight on the 31st before this Section got away, and during the struggle with the rear arc of the platform two fourteen-foot levers had been broken. All the Sections reached Gouy-Servins in time for breakfast, and two joy days were spent in the field where the Brigade and the other batteries were at " rest."

On the night of August 1st/2nd we bade farewell to the amenities of Gouy and proceeded in lorries to the railway station at Hersin. Our destination was a secret and remained so until the end of the journey. At the railway station we found 69 Siege Battery which was to share our train. As was always the case in moves of this sort, the train was very late, and we had to wait while "69," who were to load first, got their guns on the trucks. When our turn came we had a comparatively easy job, as we found there were some Tank trucks available. Each of these trucks was about forty feet long, and when they were coupled and their buffers packed with planks, a continuous way was provided which allowed our six caterpillars with the guns, platforms and limbers to run straight on. We started out of Hersin about 1.30 p.m. on August 1st, and although the train was anything but an express, it did its best to keep moving, and generally succeeded.

CHAPTER X

Forward from Amiens

[August, 1918]

Everything comes to an end in this world, and the train journey from Hersin proved no exception, in spite of prophecies to the contrary from certain restless members of the Battery who found two days' confinement in a railway truck a restraint on their energies. But if the journey seemed long, the war seemed longer, and had anyone just then made so bold as to suggest that we were about to take part in an advance which, in the short space of three months, would bring the fighting to an end, he would have been rudely laughed at as a super-optimist, and kept under close observation for further signs of incipient lunacy.

At 8 a.m. on August 3rd, the train pulled wearily into Saleux railway station, and we realised that the first part of our journey was at an end. Saleux, since the German advance, had served as the rail-head for the Amiens sector. Longeau, Boves and Amiens itself, were all within range of the enemy's guns, and it had thus become necessary to establish a rail-head well behind the line.

The spectacle presented by the railway station made the object of our journey apparent: it was evident that there was going to be a "show"—a great show—and we had been moved down for the special purpose of taking part in it. A huge amount of war material of all kinds was collected in and about the station and sidings, and trains were continuing to arrive with ordnance of every description. Big guns and little guns were unloaded side by side; tanks there were in great number, and bustle and excitement prevailed everywhere.

There was only one ramp available, and this delayed us for a time, but as soon as "69" had got their guns off, ours were unloaded very quickly, the whole business being completed in fifty-nine minutes. In the meantime the Ford car had been detrained and the Major had succeeded in finding the Brigade H.Q., which were at Boves, a village about five miles behind the front line and six miles in front of Amiens. Colonel Curteis told him of the gigantic preparations which were being made for an attack on August 8th. There was to be a big concentration of artillery, and the batteries in the 83rd Brigade were to pull into a small area in front of Gentelles Wood, so as to be in action by the night of the 7th. The greatest secrecy was to be maintained, and no movement of any kind was to take place in the area during the day, neither were the roads leading to the positions to be used except during the hours of darkness. Every trace of work done during the night was to be covered up before daybreak, and, in order to avoid anything in the nature of fires, all cooking was to be done at least five miles behind the line. The Major was also told that "135" would be required to have 1,500 rounds (250 per gun) of ammunition near the pits by the night previous to zero day.

Major Heath next hurried off to Gentelles Wood. Lieutenant Allen went with him, and together they reconnoitred the position and finally pegged out places for the six platforms. They got back to the Saleux rail-head about 6 p.m. and the Major thereupon gave orders for the three Section Commanders, Lieutenants Allen, Stevens and Hobbs, together with sixty other ranks, to set out for the position at dusk. They were to work on the pits during the night, but were to be well clear of the neighbourhood by daybreak. It was arranged that their rations should be sent to Boves, whither they were to return on leaving the position.

The working party accordingly set out from Saleux in three lorries about 9 p.m. Lieutenants Allen and Stevens, who had the only available map, piloted the first lorry. Both these officers had been to the position once by daylight, and they were supposed to know the difficult road by heart. The driver of No. 2 lorry had instructions to follow No. 1, and No. 3 lorry, in which Lieutenant Hobbs brought up the rear, was to hang on to the dust of the second lorry. Before the procession had proceeded far a traffic control interfered and turned the lorries from the direct road through Amiens which, for some reason, was closed to lorry traffic. This rendered the work of the guides anything but easy; the night was pitch dark, and it became increasingly difficult to identify the country with the map. An exciting chase ensued: no lights could be shown on the lorries, with the result that more than once No. 2 lost No. 1, and No. 3 found it extremely difficult to keep touch with No. 2. At one stage of the journey two sharp turns were taken—to the right and then again to the right almost immediately. No 2 was seen to take the first turn, but on rounding the same corner, No. 3 was unable to trace any sign of No. 2. About thirty yards farther on there were roads both to the right and left, and it became necessary to decide as to which of these No. 2 had taken. The one to the right was followed, and luckily it proved to be the correct one, as, after a feverish three or four minutes at top speed, the rear of No. 2 once more became visible. A little farther on the lorries emerged from the blackness of a road enclosed with tall trees on to a straight, but very narrow, track across pasture land so devoid of foliage that it appeared almost as a desert. Straight ahead and, indeed, on all sides could be seen the white Very lights which the enemy was accustomed to use at night. They appeared quite near; so close, in fact, that it seemed that a few more minutes must bring the lorries into the Bosche line. Actually, they were quite a long way off, as presently the road led into a village which proved to be Boves. On went the lorries past the deserted houses, which appeared uncanny in their black silence, until the edge of the village was reached. Here they came to an abrupt halt, and the officers conferred as to which was the right road to take. From the map it seemed that one leading under a railway arch was the direct route, but both Lieutenant Allen and Lieutenant Stevens were sure that no such arch had crossed their route when making the journey earlier in the day. It was finally decided to bear to the right where there seemed to be quite a good road. The lorries started off again, but only a few hundred yards had been covered when further progress was forbidden by an obstacle in the form of a brick wall! It then appeared that the road taken led only to a railway yard, a cul-de-sac out of which there was no room to turn, and whence it became necessary to back out on to the road just left. There was now no alternative but to follow the road leading under the arch, and this, after all, proved to be the right one, for after

GENTELLES WOOD POSITION.

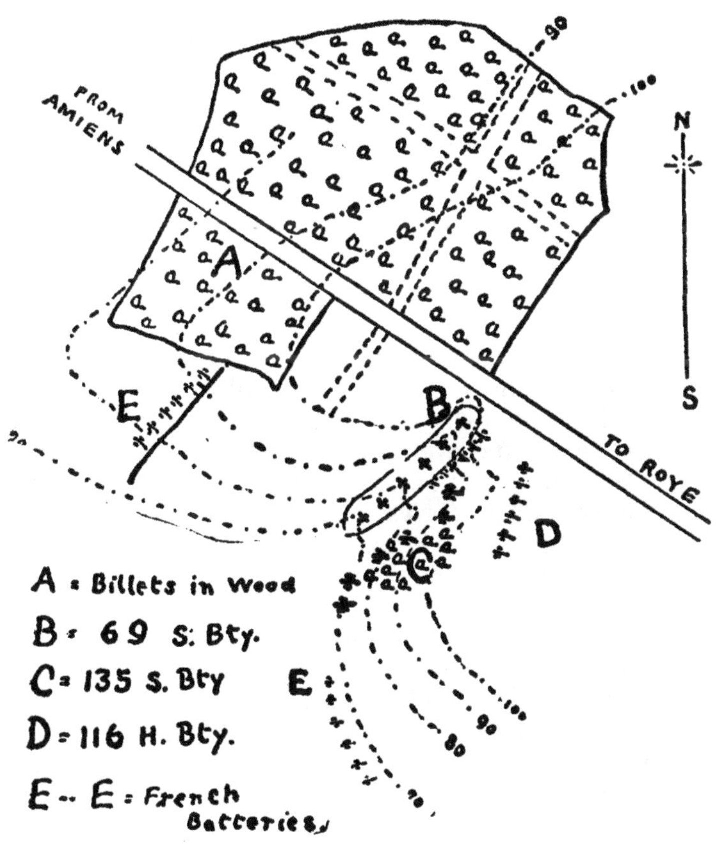

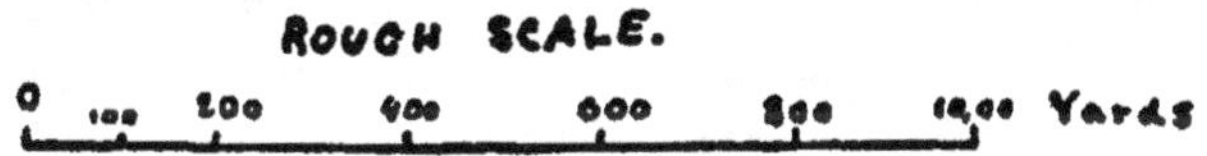

proceeding a further three miles the road led through the densely-foliaged Gentelles Wood. At the forward edge of the Wood the lorries finally halted, and the men alighted.

It was almost 3 a.m. before the various stores had been unloaded. Picks, spades, planks, levers, etc., had to be carried about 400 yards from the road into the position, and when this work had, at last, been completed, preparations were begun for the laying of the gun platforms. This was not allowed to continue without interruption, as almost as soon as a start had been made, the Hun rendered things miserably unpleasant by shelling the place with gas shells. None of the party knew anything about the position, but there seemed to be scarcely any cover. Fortunately there were no casualties, and the work was proceeded with, the enemy's fire becoming desultory as day began to break.

The places chosen for the platforms were in a wooded ravine about 400 yards to the right of the Amiens—Roye road. The pits were distributed over an area of about 200 yards and were arranged so that the guns of each Section should be close to one another, the Left Section being slightly forward of the other two. The great disadvantage of the position was difficulty of ingress and supply. The emplacements for the Centre Section were especially difficult of approach, being at the foot of a steep slope, amidst trees and bushes. The locality had formerly been used by the French Artillery, which had suffered numerous casualties while there, and had lately moved out to occupy a position slightly to the south. The enemy can be pardoned for his attention as, from the map, the position would be read as a most likely one for guns.

Work was continued on the pits until it became dangerously light, and even then very little apparent progress had been made. The ground was most difficult, being encumbered with bushes and thick undergrowth. It became urgent, however, to withdraw the party before enemy planes should begin scouting, and therefore, just before 6 a.m., the pits were camouflaged as far as was possible, and the men got together near the road to march back to Boves. It had been arranged that the party should billet in that village until dusk, when work on the position was to be continued.

The party had proceeded only a short way when shells began to burst on the road a few hundred yards in front.

The order was given to disperse into the wood which bordered the road on either side. The shelling continued at the rate of one round per minute until the party had reached the western edge of the wood. It then seemed that the firing had ceased and the men once more collected on the road. They had scarcely moved off, however, when a shell burst just in rear, and was followed immediately by another which burst in front. It appeared that the enemy was sweeping the road, but the party continued to march west, as it was impossible to guess where the next round would fall. About two minutes later a shell burst just on the left of the party, whereupon Lieutenant Allen gave the order, "Double!" so as to get the men out of what appeared to be the enemy's bracket. This timely double probably had the effect of saving the party, as the next burst was well in rear. The incident demonstrated how repugnant it is to the British Tommy to run away even when there is no object in sticking it: by the half-hearted way in which some of the men doubled it was clear that they failed to realise that the officer in charge was responsible for each of their lives, and no matter how objectionable it may have been to him to give the order to run, it was his absolute duty to do so.

After a march of three miles, the party reached Boves, which, in the bright sunlight, presented an appearance very different to the desolate village of the night before. The men were very tired, and while some gathered sticks in order to kindle a blaze and brew some tea, others fell fast asleep on the ground. In the meantime Lieutenants Allen and Stevens had gone to find the Town Major in order to secure billets. Having succeeded in arousing that dignitary from his matinal slumber, they were told that on no account could the men be allowed to remain in the village as there would be a grave risk of dysentery resulting from the impurity of the water and the plague of flies. Lieutenant Stevens then tried a little gentle persuasion, and finally succeeded in obtaining, for one day, the use of a house for the men and another for the officers.

The only thing now lacking was the rations, and these had failed to arrive. Everyone was feeling very hungry, as the last meal (which consisted only of biscuits) had been eaten about 5 p.m. on the previous day. The men were so fagged that sleep would, in the ordinary way, have rendered the absence of the rations less conspicuous, but the flies were so numerous and attentive that sleep was quite impossible.

The morning grew old but still no rations appeared. About 11.30 a.m. the Major turned up in the Ford. He found his three subalterns huddled-up on the floor of an empty house vainly endeavouring to sleep in spite of the flies. As he said afterwards, there was not much to choose between them as regards amiability: they seemed more than capable of biting each other's heads off, and unanimous as regards their desire to bite his off. Innocent as to the cause of their discomfort, the Major began a mild strafe as to the small amount of work done at the position during the night. He found, however, that his listeners were apathetic, and it was gently hinted to him that any discussion on such a topic must be postponed until they had fortified themselves with some food. Learning that the party had had nothing to eat since the previous afternoon, the Major hurried back to Saleux to send something along. The "something" arrived by the Ford about 2 p.m. It had been very eagerly awaited, and the heavy wooden box which was lifted from the car into the men's billet seemed to promise great things. Sixty-three hungry men then witnessed the removal from the box of seven small tins (single ration) of bully, twenty bottles of mixed pickles and a small bag of sultanas! It is generally acknowledged that had it not been for Tommy's sense of humour, the war would have been lost in 1914. August, 1918, found him still able to appreciate a humorous situation, and thus it was that the sixty-three hungry ones chuckled at the sight of the pickle jars. It was, perhaps, just as well that the comedian who packed the case was not within reach, as otherwise he might have received a certain amount of attention from numerous burly gunners, who found it difficult to fill a void of twenty-two hours with small pieces of pickled cauliflower.

At 6.30 p.m. the party found itself once more *en route* for the new position, and that night good progress was made in the preparation of the pits.

During the night the remainder of the Battery moved up to Gentelles Wood. Lieutenant Noakes and about fifteen gunners were left behind at the Column, just east of Vers, in order to help Lieutenant Howell in the heavy task of getting the ammunition up to the Battery. The Q.M.S., with such stores as were not likely to be required during the battle, also remained with the Column.

The days preceding August 8th will not easily be forgotten by those who were with the Battery: they were days of constant and heavy strain. The nights, if anything, were worse, as it was during darkness that most of the laborious work in the position had to be carried out. It rained almost incessantly, and this added to the discomfort of every one: the heavy traffic on the Amiens-Roye road soon cut up the surface and the Battery position became a quagmire. This greatly retarded progress, and the labour of conveying the shell from the road to the guns—a distance of 400 yards—was increased fourfold. Fifteen hundred rounds of 8-inch shell weigh approximately 134 tons, and the whole of this had to be unloaded from the road and taken to the position by hand. All kinds of ruses were tried. At first drag-ropes were attached to the plug eyes and the rounds dragged singly through the mud. This method proving too slow, planks were resorted to. These were laid down from the road into the position and the shell rolled along them. Better progress was made in this way, but the planks had to be taken up each day before it was light and safely hidden from the enemy's planes until dusk when they had to be relaid. August 7th still found the work very much in arrear, and we were despairing of being able to get the full supply to the guns, when three G.S. wagons were detailed to our use and by means of these it became just possible to complete the supply in time for the battle.

Words cannot adequately express the splendid work done by all ranks during this very trying period. The men's clothes were soaked with rain most of the time, and the few hours rest which they were occasionally allowed were spent in a wood reeking with damp and without the comfort of a fire of any sort. The officers had to be on duty practically without a break, as Lieutenants Curtis and Hooper were on leave in England and Lieutenant Allen had been temporarily taken from the Battery and attached to Brigade Headquarters. To make matters worse, on August 6th, Captain Phillips was detailed to take charge of an ammunition dump and his very valuable services were thus lost to the Battery for the time being.

As August 8th drew near every one became supremely

confident. This was doubtlessly due to the huge concentration of arms of all description which seemed to make success a certainty. The weather, which had been a very doubtful neutral on the occasions of former attacks, cleared up on the night of the 6th, and the 7th was a fine day with plenty of sun which helped to dry up the ground.

The Canadian Corps were to attack immediately in front of us with the Australians on their left and the French on their right. Forty-four batteries of Heavy Artillery were attached to the Canadians besides a large number of field batteries. Those which had been in the area for some time continued their ordinary daily shoots as if circumstances were normal, but the newly arrived batteries were not allowed to fire until the launching of the attack, and consequently no registration could be carried out. The lines of fire were laid out with great care. The Field Survey Section resected a point about a mile south of the position and placed a flag there for the use of all batteries in the neighbourhood. Another flag was placed at another resected spot about 200 yards in rear of the position, and the position of one of the guns was also resected. This enabled the guns to be layed with great accuracy.

On the evening of the 7th Operation Orders came through from Brigade. Zero hour was fixed as 4.20 a.m. on August 8th. The Battery's task was to neutralise six hostile batteries (one gun on each) and to take part at intervals in certain concentrations on places where the enemy would be likely to assemble troops. The counter-battery targets were to be bombarded until the Field Artillery barrage came within 600 yards of each location, when the gun on that target would cease and lift to a more distant target. In addition we had to supply an officer to man one of the Brigade O.P.'s. Lieutenant T. R. Wood was detailed for this job and took with him two signallers. The personnel was distributed as follows :—

B.C. Post.—The Battery Commander and Lieutenant Gill.

Left Section.	*Centre Section.*	*Right Section.*
Lieut C R. H. Hobbs.	Lieut. Stevens.	Lieut. W. R. Jones.
E. & F. Sub-Sections.	C. & D. Sub-Sections.	A. & B. Sub-Sections.
(Sergts. Baldwin and Morley).	(Sergts. Branch and Marsh).	(Sergts. Darby and Lockley).

Watches were synchronised by Corps H.A. during the evening of the 7th, and 10 p.m. found the Major busy in the B.C. post working out the targets. The Section

Commanders were engaged with their sections in seeing that everything was in readiness for the morrow, while the detachments for the most part were endeavouring to clean the mud from the shell.

There was much speculation as to whether the enemy was still ignorant of the little affair we were so thoughtfully arranging for him ; it seemed hardly possible for his airmen to have noticed nothing of the heavy preparations of the last few days. In the event of his having acquired information of the impending attack, it was thought that he would probably drench our lines with gas during the night. In order to neutralise such measures the guns were given special targets on which to open in the event of a gas bombardment.

The Amiens—Roye road about 1 a.m. on the 8th presented a sight never to be forgotten. It was crowded with transport of every description making the last journey to the line. Stores to meet every conceivable need were moving slowly forward: ammunition for the infantry, medical stores, rations and everything which a perfect organisation could provide. Nothing had been forgotten, as witnessed the G.S. waggon laden with sign posts ready to be stuck into the ground and on which were already painted the names of the villages which it was hoped would be taken during the advance. Plenty of cavalry and numerous tanks were also to be seen making for their respective points of assembly.

Shortly before zero hour the gun detachments, which had been working all night, were relieved by fresh detachments from Gentelles Wood. About 4 a.m. the guns were layed on the targets on which they were to open fire. The much-dreaded gas defence of the enemy had not materialised. At 4.15 the section officers had their ears glued to the telephones just in rear of their sections. At 4.18 the order came down from the Battery Commander, " Stand by for salvo." The numbers 2 of each gun stood grasping the lanyard, and keeping their eyes fixed on the section officer waiting for the signal to fire. At 4.19 the front was so still that . . . Crash ! Boom—m—m—m ! the sound was deafening ; the whole front was ablaze ; it seemed as if hell itself had been let loose. In front, the first wave of infantry (which had actually been over the top and halfway across no man's land a few seconds before zero), had already reached the Hun and were dealing with him gracefully. Tanks, armoured cars and machine guns were all going forward. The Field Artillery barrage was being adjusted every few minutes to enable the troops to make their rapid advance. To all this the thunder of the heavy howitzers and the crack of the guns supplied an appropriate accompaniment. The enemy, taken entirely by surprise, was running as fast as he could and several of the first batch of prisoners were taken in their pyjamas. The early morning mist, which had aided our troops considerably, was soon intensified by the smoke of the bombardment. Our planes were keeping touch with the infantry as far as possible and were sending back news of the progress.

In the meantime work in the Battery went forward without a hitch. The Battery Commander was kept busy in giving fresh targets to the Section Commanders, and the gun detachments were quick to realise that the increased elevations which were being constantly given to the pieces meant that things were going well.

The Bosche gunners made only a feeble reply and seem to have devoted themselves at once to the withdrawal of their guns. The Centre and Left Sections each received a few rounds, but they caused no damage and we suffered no casualties.

About 6 a.m. the first batch of prisoners began to stream back from the line. A cage had been provided for these gentlemen some way back on the Amiens—Roye road. It certainly did not possess " every modern convenience," but even the Hun could not complain that we had stinted him as regards barbed wire.

At 9.20 a.m. the task of the Battery was finished. The enemy had retreated out of range! So fast had he run and so energetic had been the pursuit, that there was no definite news as to what points had been reached. The six guns had fired in all 700 rounds, which means that the Hun received from 135 S.B. alone, sixty-two tons of high explosive shell.

About 10 a.m., Colonel Curteis, the Brigade Commander, rode into the position and visited each section. He was evidently feeling pleased as a result of the morning's work, and addressed some very encouraging words to the detachments, congratulating them on their splendid work in getting into position in such a short time and under such extraordinarily adverse conditions. He said that the heavy work which they had put in had undoubtedly helped

A Detachment of the Battery Serving a Gun in Action, May, 1917.

to make victory possible, and while he doubted if any other men could have done as well, he knew that none could have done better.

About 12.30 p.m. Brigade rang through to the Major and informed him that some German guns had been captured in Hamon Wood and asked him to send a party up to man them so that they might be brought to bear on the retreating Hun. Major Heath detailed Lieutenant Hobbs to go to the billet position to collect thirty volunteers from the detachments that had come off duty before the battle opened. No difficulty was experienced in raising the required number, and when the Major appeared a few minutes later some of the men who had been left out made a special appeal to be included. Finally, about thirty-four started out under Lieutenant Hobbs. The Major went on in the car and on reaching Hamon Wood found that there were numerous captured guns there. One slim looking creature, a 10-c.m. gun, seemed likely to provide the greatest amount of amusement, and having chalked 135 S.B. on the piece, the Major then went on in the car along the Roye road to learn how things were going. Presently he found an Infantry Brigade H.Q. in a dug-out south of the road which was being whizz-banged in a somewhat unhealthy way. The Brigadier told him that the infantry were being held up on the western outskirts of Le Quesnel and that he would be glad of fire on the village. Returning to Hamon Wood Major Heath found that the party from the Battery had arrived, but were somewhat worn out after a five-mile march. The 10-c.m. gun was run out of the wood on to a hard piece of ground just near the road. A manuscript range table had been found and with the aid of this, fire was opened on Le Quesnel with plenty of "safety" on. The sighting arrangements were somewhat of a puzzle, but Corporal Harding made an excellent No. 4, and received plenty of advice from thirty-three other gunners. When Colonel Curteis arrived on the scene a few minutes later the gun was being fired at the rate of three rounds per minute. The Colonel was highly gratified at this cheery sight and the reserves of infantry going up the line seemed to think it splendid fun. "Put 'em over, boys," shouted one wit, "I'll tell yer what yer haven't hit when I get there." About 7 p.m., the Major went back to the Battery to see what was happening there. Lieutenant Hobbs was left in charge of the gun and continued firing until it was dark. The men then endeavoured to make themselves comfortable for an hour or two in the wood. About 10 p.m. a special dispatch rider appeared from Brigade with firing orders for the officer in charge of the gun. The dispatch intimated that a counter-attack was expected and ordered fire to be directed on Vrély and Warvilliers, two villages about 13,000 yards distant. Sufficient men were roused to man the gun and firing was carried out at intervals throughout the night. The expected counter-attack did not materialise, however, and the following day, about 11.30 a.m., Lieutenant Hobbs was relieved by Lieutenant Gill. The further history of the gun can best be gathered from the following extracts which are taken from Major Heath's diary:

"9th August.—Noakes came back from the column and took over Phillips's job as O.C. ammunition dump. I decided to put Phillips in charge of the 10-c.m. Bosche gun with Gill to assist him, and about midday went up to Hamon Wood to see what was doing, leaving orders that the detachments were to dig round their platforms in order that they might be able to take them up quickly if required. On arriving at the 10-c.m. gun, I found that it was now out of range, so decided to advance it. The difficulty was transport. All our lorries had been taken out of my hands and were employed in assisting in the supply of ammunition to the 6-inch and 60-pounder batteries which had advanced. However, going on a bit, I luckily found the two 6-inch batteries halted near Beaucourt with all their, and some of our, transport. They were naturally very loath to part with any of it as they did not know when they were to go forward, but after some begging I managed to borrow two lorries from them and took these back to the 10-c.m. gun. Phillips and Gill had by now arrived. We hitched the 10-c.m. gun on behind one of the lorries, loaded the men and as much ammunition as we could, and rolled off to a position I had found behind the road north of Fresnoy-en-Chausée, west of Le Quesnel. On our way we passed one of the 60-pounder batteries who, up to then, fancied themselves as being the forward battery of the Brigade, but they were not in it now. We ran the gun into an old Hun battery position, the pits and shelters of which would be useful for our men, and began to think about targets. There was no map available, so all we could do was to use the one map which the 60-pounder battery had, measure certain angles and ranges from it and keep a note of them at the 10-c.m. position. We connected up by phone to the 60-pounder battery, and were thus in communication with Brigade, who gave us a target that evening. I left Phillips in charge of the gun and returned to the Battery. . . .

"12th August.—I went up to see Phillips and found that he had moved the Bosche gun to a position on the road about half a mile south of Folies, and had got it under a large tree together with another of the same calibre which had recently been captured from the Hun. As he had not registered we decided to see what we could do. A small factory chimney on the main road at Bouchoir served as an O.P., but our registration was not successful as the distance was too great to observe rounds which gave such a small burst. . . .

"16th August.—The Brigade arranged for the collection of a number of captured guns, and Captain Phillips was put in charge of a battery of 5·9-inch howitzers in position near Rouvroy. Lieutenant Gill had charge of a collection of 10-c.m. guns (including the two which we had been using since August 8th) in an advanced position south of Rouvroy. He fired constantly and did some excellent work. The personnel for these Bosche batteries was drawn from various batteries in the Brigade."

We must apologise for having made this digression in favour of the history of the Bosche guns, but it was an experience which fell to the lot of few batteries and there was a certain amount of pleasure in sending back some of the enemy's ammunition through the medium of his own guns.

It will be remembered that the Battery had been left resting contentedly after its programme of August 8th. On the night of the 9th, the Battery pulled out of its late position and started its advance with that splendid Army which never again looked back until the Hun was beaten. Hamon Wood was reached on the 10th. A halt was made there which lasted two days, but no firing was done, as almost as soon as the guns had arrived the enemy was once more out of range. On the 12th the Major went to Brigade H.Q. at Beaufort. He then received orders that the Battery was to move up that night and park on the main road south of Le Quesnel, so as to be ready to go into action on the next night just north of Folies. He got back to the Battery about 9 p.m. and at 9.30 p.m. the men fell in for the move. The starting off was made unpleasant by numerous enemy planes which hovered over the road dropping bombs, but the Battery had its usual good luck and managed to dodge these. The neighbourhood of Le Quesnel was reached at 12.30 a.m. on the 13th, and we camped for the night in a field near the main road. The next morning we started off again and reached Folies at 9 a.m.

The gun positions were chosen and digging parties commenced their work on the trenches for the platforms. The guns of the Right Section, under Lieutenant Jones, were hidden in a small hollow on the western outskirts of the village; while the other two sections commenced work on an old French position which had more recently been used by the Hun: it was about seven hundred yards north of Folies and in open country, but there was good cover for the detachments.

The platforms of all guns were laid on the morning of the 13th on a centre line bearing of 90° Grid, but no sooner had the work been completed than a message came through from Brigade to the effect that the centre line bearing should have been 125° Grid. This necessitated the undoing of all the work that had been done, and it was almost dark before the platforms had been taken up and relaid at the new bearing. We were not, however, at the end of our troubles, for scarcely had the men settled down for the night when yet another message came through from Brigade. This time it was to inform the Battery Commander that the Grid bearing of 125° had been cancelled, and that the platforms were to be put back on their original centre line bearing of 90°. The British Tommy has been accused of being undemonstrative. As a generalisation this may, or may not, be true, but the most unobservant "special correspondent with the forces" could hardly have failed on this occasion to notice that the worthy gunners of "135" were anything but undemonstrative. The whole affair was really rather heartbreaking, and it required a somewhat strained sense of humour to get a laugh out of what appeared to be a blunder, but towards the early hours of the morning, when the work in the various pits was, for the third time, nearing completion, some wit was responsible for the following:

" Sing a song of Platforms,
 And funny Red-tabbed Dolts,
Five and fifty gunners
 And fifteen hundred bolts;
We took 'em up and put 'em down
 And took 'em up for fun,
And then we put 'em down again
 To show we wasn't done!

Sing a song of Orders,
 We've had only three,
P'raps we'll get another
 If we 'wait and see.'
Who's hard up for Bearings,
 We should like to know!
We have only had two
 And there're Three, Six, O!

Sing a song of wheel plates,
 Arcs and side-beams too,
Levers—five to fourteen feet
 And nuts that will not screw.
When the war is over
 And we are 'disengaged.'
This work on Comic Platforms
 Will fit us for the Stage!"

When the work was completed the detachments crept stealthily to their quarters, scarcely daring to speak lest it should be noised abroad that the platforms were once more planted and a change in the bearing ordered in consequence.

Lieutenant Jones's Section was even more unfortunate as, after wrestling with their platforms as described above, it was suggested by Head-quarters it would be better to have the six guns in line, and this necessitated yet another move in order to bring their guns up on the right of the other two sections. It is only fair to mention here that the alteration in the bearing of the platforms was not due to a mistake, but was necessitated by some contingency which had to be met by the Corps. Colonel Curteis visited the Battery on the following day and explained this to the men, making it quite clear that it was no one's fault, and quite unavoidable.

The period August 15th to 19th was a comparatively quiet one for the Battery. Several local attacks were made on the Hun during this period, but without any startling success.

On August 20th, Lieutenant Stevens was taken ill with what turned out to be a serious form of dysentery. Whether he contracted this at Boves earlier in the month, or whether it resulted from other causes, was not known. He was sent home to England, and to our great regret was never able to rejoin the Battery. We thus lost a very able officer, and one whose subtle wit had often been responsible for livening up dull moments in the officers' mess.

While the Battery was still in position near Folies, the French took over that part of the line which we were covering. It was arranged, however, that our allies should have the assistance of the batteries in the 83rd Brigade. L'Artillerie Lourde XXXI had their Headquarters at Hangest, and it was to this Corps that the 83rd Brigade, under Colonel Curteis, was posted as from August 21st.

CHAPTER XI

With the French Before Ham

[August–September, 1918]

The Commander of the French Corps, Colonel Florentin, soon discovered that the "Brigade Anglaise" was a very active one, and he at once proceeded to make good use of it.

A large amount of harassing fire was carried out, and there were one or two prepared attacks which finally brought about a further retirement of the enemy on the night of August 26th and 27th.

On the 27th the 6-inch howitzer and 60-pounder batteries of the Brigade advanced towards Fresnoy; "135" and the 9·2-inch battery were, however, left behind. Major Heath was anything but pleased at being forced to remain idle, and would probably plead this as an excuse for the little excursion of which the following details appear in his diary:

> "August 27th.—I took one of the motor-bikes and rode up to the O.P., which was then manned by Lieutenant Allen. The Hun had retired out of sight of this, so I rode on to Fresnoy, and, leaving the bike there, proceeded on foot towards Liancourt. I met, on the way, various parties of Frenchmen who seemed to know little about the situation (or perhaps they did not understand my French!). I avoided Liancourt as it was being strafed and went north of it. I noticed that the country here was completely deserted, and began to feel a bit uncomfortable when I met a patrol of five French infantrymen, who instantly levelled their rifles at me. After some difficulty I managed to convince them that I was not a Hun, and joined their party. They seemed rather vague as to where the Huns were, but I presumed they knew roughly, and apparently they thought I knew! In this condition we progressed along a wide, bare stretch north of Liancourt. Then, quite close in

front of us, we heard machine-gun fire apparently coming from a wood on our left, and later saw some French infantry running to take cover. However, we went on a bit till the Hun machine gunners thought we were close enough, when they opened fire on us at about five hundred yards. We scattered pretty quickly. The Frenchmen ran to the left, but I thought it best to lie flat in the grass. The Huns had evidently spotted me as an officer, for they kept playing about me whenever I moved. It was somewhat uncomfortable, and it was only after I had crawled some five hundred yards that I reached a sunken road north of Liancourt! I lost sight of the Frenchmen and never knew whether any of them were hit."

On August 30th Brigade Head-quarters and the more mobile batteries were in the Nesle area, and the Major decided to take an advance party with him and camp near Brigade Head-quarters so that, when required, an immediate start could be made on a new position. He left Captain Phillips in charge of the Battery and took with him Lieutenants Allen and Curtis, and thirty other ranks. It was not, at the time, expected that the Battery would be required to move up for at least a day or two, but it seems that the unexpected happened. We will once more quote from the Major's diary:

"August 30th.—. . . We arrived at the camping-place on the road just west of Rethonvillers. I am afraid we were counting on a comfortable night. I left Allen and the party preparing supper and the bivouacs, and went to report our arrival at Brigade Head-quarters, which were about a mile away. The Colonel was discussing the situation with a French Staff officer. I reported myself and the arrival of my party. The Colonel turning to the French officer said: 'Now, here's the Commander of my 8-inch Battery, would you like them to come up?' 'That would be most interesting,' said the Frenchman politely. Bang went our dreams of a quiet night in bed, for the Battery was ordered up that night! I shall always remember the look of dismay on the faces of the happy camping party when I broke the news to them that they were to pack up immediately and come on for an all-night shift."

The new position was in a valley south of the Etalon road, about three hundred yards west of Herly. A party under Lieutenant Allen was set to dig trenches for the platforms, and the Major, having secured billets in a ruined château about three hundred yards N.W. of the position, hurried back to the Battery which was sixteen miles to the rear. Arriving there at 11 p.m., he found every one had turned in and the sleepy-heads had to be roused. Captain Phillips was unwell and was left behind to bring up the rear party in the morning. The bulk of the men started off soon after midnight. The Major took them forward in lorries, and the guns were got on to the road under Lieutenant Gill. The road, in places, was badly damaged by shell-fire, especially in the neighbourhood of Cremery, but the lorries reached Herly just before dawn and the guns about 9 a.m. All sections were in action on the 31st soon after midday. It was moves of this rapidity that seemed to astonish the French. Lieutenant Hobbs, who was acting as Brigade liaison officer with the Artillerie Lourde, was constantly interrogated by the French Commander as to how these moves were so speedily accomplished. On one occasion Colonel Curteis was asked to send back information concerning the state of the roads by which his batteries had advanced, so that it might be passed down for the use of the French batteries!

While in position at Herly, the Battery was not shelled much, but the enemy did a lot of night bombing. There were, however, various cellars and dug-outs in and about the château, and no casualties were suffered. The O.P.'s were interesting, and though there was not much opportunity for observed shooting, a certain amcunt of calibration and registration was carried out.

The Brigade had an O.P. in a tree south of Languevoisin, but this was an uncomfortable place and did not command a very extensive view of the country. Major Heath and Lieutenant Allen explored the northern part of Nesle one morning and finally succeeded in finding a much better place in a little row of cottages on the hill north of the railway station. A telephone line was run out from the Battery, and Lieutenant Allen manned this new O.P. the next day. The Major looked in during the morning, and as there was nothing much to do, he and Lieutenant Allen went forward to reconnoitre. As they were returning to the O.P., the enemy started shelling it with a battery of 8-inch howitzers. They waited at a safe distance until the shelling had ceased, and then made for the spot, in some fear as to what had happened to the signallers who had been left there under Bombardier Wickenden. They found them with their instrument in a trench close to the house, the party having remained at their post throughout the shelling which had been particularly close and heavy. The O.P. itself had been struck, and it became necessary to look round for another. About half a mile N.E., at a point S.E. of Mesnil-St.-Nicaise, a nice little house was selected, which proved a good O.P. though it was a long way from the Battery. The Major and Lieutenant Jones went there the next day and calibrated some of the guns on a château in Matigny, but the Hun soon spotted the O.P. and put over several nasty concentrations of 10-c.m. and 77-mm. He did no harm, however, and failed to hit the house.

The other batteries in the Brigade were all working very hard at this period, and the 6-inch and 60-pounders were being pushed forward at the least sign of a withdrawal on the part of the enemy. 284 S.B., a battery of six 6-inch howitzers, were very unlucky. Their officers' quarters were smashed in one night by a gas shell, and unfortunately all the officers were so near as to become casualties. Lieutenant Galbraith, who was well known to "135," was among the unfortunate ones. He died a few days later from the effect of gas poisoning: a braver or more cheery soul one could not possibly have wished to meet. This unfortunate incident caused a change in the officers of "135," as Captain Phillips was given command of 284 S.B. The Battery felt this loss acutely. Phillips was the best of good fellows, and a thoroughly efficient soldier. He was whole-heartedly respected by the detachments, and his keenness as a disciplinarian no more than equalled his efforts to promote the comfort of those under him. After a good deal of persuasion he prevailed on the Major to allow Corporal D. Allan to go with him to his new command, to take charge of the "284" signallers. Allan was a splendid fellow in every sense—a brave soldier and a good signaller. His move was to gain him promotion to the rank of Sergeant, and Major Heath felt he could not stand in his way; so two of the old firm went off together.

On September 5th the 83rd Brigade left the French Corps and pulled out to go to rest at Amiens. The French Commander could not speak too highly of the "Brigade Anglaise," and was very lavish in his praise of its gallant

Colonel and all his batteries. In replying to these very courteous observations of the French officer, Lieutenant Hobbs referred only to the high respect in which the French Artillery was held by British gunners: he was sorely tempted to add his own high appreciation of the six-course *déjeuner* which he had helped to demolish daily while with the French, and the Battery bully beef to which he was returning loomed very much in his thoughts as he finally took leave.

CHAPTER XII

SEVEN DAYS' REST

[SEPTEMBER, 1918]

September 6th found the Battery at Le Quesnel, *en route* for Amiens. Captain Hickson, who had been posted to the Battery in place of Captain (now Major) Phillips, joined us there. The next day we started off again and reached Amiens late in the afternoon. The city was still minus most of its inhabitants, but there were certain signs of activity which suggested that the good shopkeepers would soon be taking down their shutters. That doleful appearance which so impressed itself on one just before our great advance in August, was beginning to disappear.

The Battery was quartered at the western outskirts of the city. Some billets were found for the men in a brewery. They were quite good although the brewery itself was absolutely "dry." The atmosphere, however, was stimulating, and one had to be satisfied with that. The officers' billets were in a school, which possessed an excellent hall with a large stage. Three very good concerts were arranged during our short stay, at which several of the members of the Battery performed creditably. During the day, the hall served admirably as a badminton court. Most of the Battery's transport was being overhauled, but by using the few lorries at his disposal, the Major managed to arrange several joy rides to Abbeville. It is feared that only about one half of the Battery were fortunate enough to participate in these, but on the whole, every one had a very good time.

The Café de la Paix was the first eating-place to resume business. There was no supply of electricity for lighting purposes, but candles stuck in empty liqueur bottles did just as well, and the enterprising proprietor had the honour of entertaining the Battery officers to dinner more than once. On the second occasion, Lieutenant ———, having sampled every vintage produced by mine host and partaken somewhat freely of a special liqueur prepared by the Major out of cigar ash, mustard and coffee, composed a brand new edition of "Beware of Chu Chin Chow," in which the hero—a robber—contrived to mistake Chinese Orient for Chinese sentiment in much the same way as Lieutenant —— had mistaken the Yellow X mustard liqueur for Chartreuse.

The Battery had enjoyed this rest for exactly a week when we were again ordered into the line. On September 14th, the officers had arranged a badminton tournament, and Lieutenant Curtis, who was running the mess, had provided something special in the way of a feed. The first round of the tournament was barely completed when an orderly arrived from Brigade with a dispatch instructing the Major to report at H.Q. This proved the end of the tournament. At 8 o'clock the Major was still absent, and it was decided to start grub without him. The much-coveted dishes had just made their appearance on the table when Major Heath blew in like a whirlwind. He wouldn't look at the magnificent bowl of salad which we were just attacking, but said something about there being no time for dinner as the Battery was to be on the road in half an hour. In vain the hungry subalterns (inspired, no doubt, by the decision in Drake *v.* The Spanish Armada) suggested that there was time to finish this "bowl" (of salad) and lick the Germans too! The Major decided to leave nothing to chance and finally said: "Every one must be out of here in ten minutes!"

The Battery was actually on the road at 9.15 p.m., under orders to proceed to the St. Quentin area by the Amiens—Vermand road. Having seen the Battery move off, the Major went on ahead in the side-car to Rainecourt where the first halt was to be made. He found that several other batteries were arriving and that there was scarcely anything to be had in the way of billets. However, when the major portion of the Battery arrived in lorries about 2 a.m. on the 15th, they managed to distribute themselves in some old dug-outs. The caterpillars, with guns and platforms, under Lieutenants Curtis and Hobbs, did not arrive until 6.30 a.m., considerable delay having occurred at Longeau, where a gun had to be picked up from the Ordnance workshop.

About 8.30 a.m. on September 16th, the Major set out

in the car, and, having succeeded in finding the Brigade Commander, he learnt the approximate locations of the position the Battery was to occupy. All batteries in the Brigade, with the exception of 69 S.B., were to pull into the valley between the village of Attilly and the St. Quentin Wood. 69 S.B. were to be slightly to the rear, on the road north of the village. The Battery's guns, with 1,500 rounds of ammunition, were to be in position on the night of September 17th for an attack on the German positions at an early hour the next day. The locality had a bad reputation, and the Hun was putting up a very determined resistance. As events turned out the position proved one of the most unpleasant that the Battery ever occupied, and it would be inappropriate to include our doings there in the same chapter as records our delightful stay at Amiens.

CHAPTER XIII

Attilly

[September, 1918]

The Major reached the new position about midday on September 15th, and having had instructions to occupy the extreme south of the Brigade area, finally decided to distribute the guns as in the diagram on the next page. By keeping the sections as far apart as possible it was hoped to minimise the danger of the whole Battery being neutralised at the same time. The two guns of the Right Section were concealed in a quarry just north of the Attilly-St. Quentin road, and about two hundred yards west of them some bushes, enclosing a portion of the Vermand-St. Quentin railway, afforded some slight cover for the Centre Section. The two guns of the Left Section were to pull in on the south of the road separating the St. Quentin and Holnon Woods, suitable clearings for the platforms being found on the western edge of a small and sparsely-wooded copse. The Major decided to billet the Battery just south of Villeveque, a village about 2½ miles west of the fighting position. This would allow all detachments off duty to make themselves more comfortable, and to get their meals properly cooked.

It will be remembered that the Battery was still at Rainecourt. Major Heath sent back instructions for Lieutenants Wood and Gill to hurry forward with a working party so that work might be started at the position that night. The guns were to advance to Mons-en-Chausée and the remainder of the Battery were to bring the gun stores up to the fighting position in lorries, and then retire to the billets at Villeveque.

Lieutenants Wood and Gill, with their party, arrived at the position just before dark, and work was at once commenced on digging trenches for the platforms. It was anything but enjoyable. The enemy shelled the

ATTILLY.

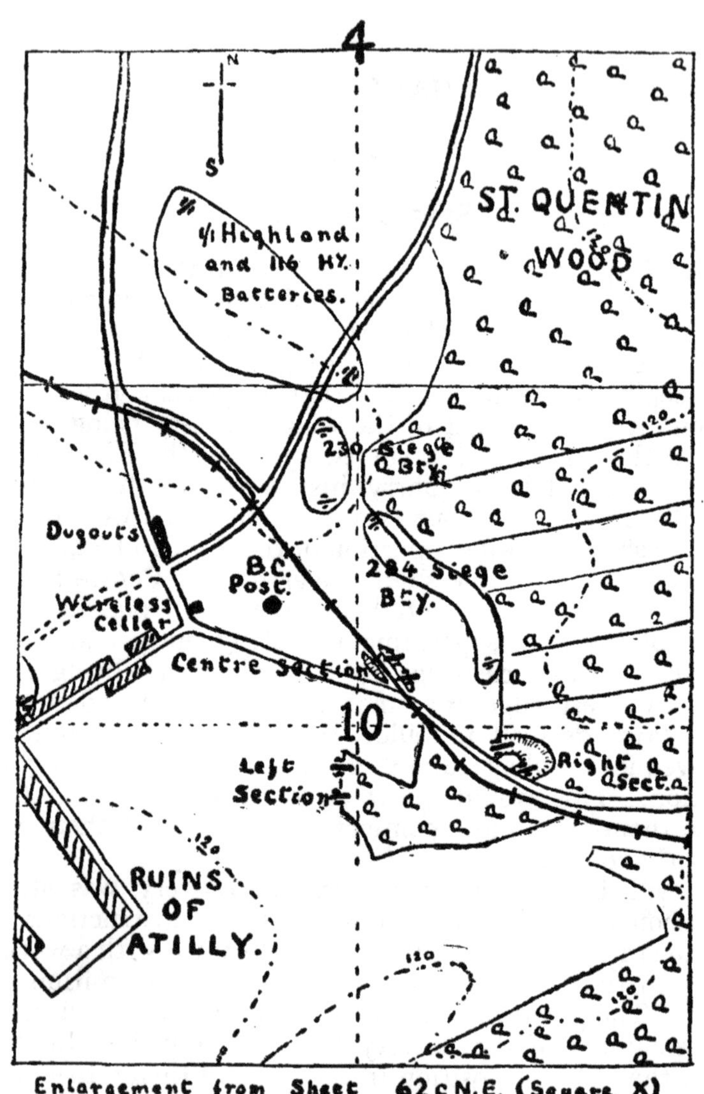

Enlargement from Sheet 62c N.E. (Square X)
Scale $\frac{1}{10,000}$. Squares, 500 Yds.

neighbourhood steadily from 8 p.m. until just before daybreak on the 16th. 284 Siege Battery, which was immediately on our left, came in for a heavy concentration about 10.30 p.m. The shelling was all round them, but, under Major Phillips, they continued their task of pulling in. They had several casualties, and a driver of one of their F.W.D.'s was killed. We also suffered two casualties. Bombardier Lancaster, who has already been mentioned for the good work he did on March 28th, was hit while working with Lieutenant Wood's party. His wound was not thought to be serious and he was sent back on foot to a dressing station. It seems that he had only gone a short distance when he received another wound from a shell which landed quite close to him. He lay in the open unnoticed for several hours, before being picked up by some men belonging to another unit. Lancaster managed to recover, but unfortunately one of his legs had to be amputated. Early on the morning of the 16th, Corporal Harding was hit and went to hospital. He did not rejoin us until after the armistice. This was the third occasion on which this very efficient N.C.O. was wounded while with the Battery.

About 1 a.m. on the 16th, the lorries with the gun stores arrived at the position under Lieutenants Allen and Hobbs. They had been on the road since the early afternoon of the day previous, having been delayed considerably owing to the crowded state of the roads. Lieutenant Howell, R.A.S.C., came with them. After the stores had been unloaded, this party was taken by the Major to the billet position to get a night's rest, as most of the men comprising it had been on the road during the whole of the preceding night, bringing the guns from Amiens. When Villeveque was reached it was discovered that neither rations nor bivouac sheets had been brought with the stores. One of the lorries, containing, as it was thought, only Q.M. stores, had been left behind with the Column at Athies, and it now appeared that rations and tents must have been included in its load. As the men had had nothing to eat for more than twelve hours, Lieutenant Allen volunteered to take the car back to the Column and retrieve the lost rations. The men, however, were too tired to wait about for biscuits and very wisely settled down as comfortably as they could under some trees. The Ford arrived back some two hours later looking very much like a travelling circus. After removing several bundles of "bivvy" sheets and numerous boxes of bully beef, the unloading party came across Lieutenant Allen. He was fast asleep and so beautifully snug that he was quite offended at being wakened.

The party which had been working at the position all night, returned to Villeveque as soon as it was light, and at about 8.30 a.m. another party, under Lieutenants Allen and Hobbs, set out from the billets to carry on the work at the position. They were severely shelled during the greater part of the time, and no work could be done on the Left Section, which was cut off by gas shelling during the whole day. In the afternoon Brigadier-General G. B. Mackenzie, C.M.G., D.S.O., the G.O.C., H.A., visited the position and seemed especially pleased that the 8-inch howitzers were in front of the Field Artillery! Lieutenant Allen, although feeling inwardly that there was no particular reason to jump for joy over this, made a brave attempt to agree with all the General said. The latter was very friendly and strongly advised getting the working party under cover during the bursts of fire which the enemy was putting over. At dusk Lieutenant Allen's party was relieved by another, under Lieutenants Curtis and T. R. Wood. Major Heath was also in the position during most of the night. The shelling continued, but was not quite so near, and good progress was made. The platforms arrived about 1 a.m., and the work of laying them was almost complete when the detachments returned to Villeveque at dawn.

About 9 a.m. on the 17th Lieutenants Allen and Hobbs again took their party to the position. The platforms were completed, and Lieutenant Allen superintended the construction of a small B.C. Post. While this was going on, Lieutenant Hobbs employed the remainder of the party on the task of digging slit trenches for the Left Section. One was started for each gun, and later on in the day when the personnel proper to the section arrived, the work was energetically continued. After-events proved that these trenches were responsible for saving the lives of many of the section.

Lieutenant Curtis, O/C Signals, was busy during the whole of the 17th looking after the communications. The B.C. Post was connected up with Brigade H.Q., and each section was linked up in telephonic communication with the B.C. Post. During the day Lieutenant Jones, who had been detailed to bring the guns up from Mons-en-Chaussée, arrived with them somewhere in the neighbourhood of Villeveque. As soon as it was dark they were brought up to the position and put on to the platforms.

On the evening of the 17th everything was ready in the Battery, but there was still some ammunition to be got into the sections to complete the 250 rounds per gun. The ammunition dump from which we drew was established at the cross-roads east of Trefcon. This was some way back, and just at the time there was a serious shortage of lorries in the Brigade. Moreover, all roads at night were very crowded with slow-moving traffic. Lieutenant Howell made every effort to ensure that we should have every round that could be got to the Battery. The R.A.S.C. attached to other batteries in the Brigade were experiencing an equally bad time. The whole area was so unhealthy, and the shell holes so numerous, that some drivers had hesitated to risk their lorries. As a consequence, each battery in the Brigade was ordered to detail an Artillery officer to accompany the lorries on the road. Major Heath detailed Lieutenant Gill for this somewhat thankless job. Lieutenant Howell was naturally rather hurt at what seemed to be a reflection on the Column, and in this particular case the provision was quite uncalled for, as he had his drivers working splendidly. As a result of much hard work during the early hours of the 18th the full supply of ammunition was got to each section.

The Battery was suffering from a serious shortage of officers at this period. It has already been recorded that Lieutenant Hooper had been taken ill while on leave, and it will be remembered that Lieutenant Stevens had been obliged to leave us while we were at Folies. Captain Hickson and Lieutenant Noakes had both gone on leave while we were at Amiens. The Battery Commander now had at his disposal Lieutenants Allen, Curtis, Jones, Wood, Gill and Hobbs. Lieutenant Gill was wholly occupied with the Column, and the others were distributed as follows :

Left Section.	Centre Section.	Right Section.
Lieut. Hobbs.	Lieut. T. R. Wood.	Lieut. Allen.

Signals Officer—Lieut. Curtis.
O.P. Officer—Lieut. Jones.

Lieutenant Jones had been detailed by the O.C. to do all O.P. work. The carrying out of this duty by one officer helped to promote far greater efficiency in this very important branch of our work. In an advance, where the probabilities are against the Battery remaining in the same position for more than a few days, there are but small opportunities for several officers to become acquainted with the country as seen from the O.P., and changing the Forward Observation Officer on each successive day means that many hours must be wasted by the new F.O.O. before he can gain a thorough knowledge of the country before him.

Lieutenant Jones carried out his duties most efficiently. He was allowed very little rest, as every other day he had a tour of duty lasting twenty-four hours, as Brigade F.O.O. On the nights that he was lucky enough to be off duty, he slept at the billet at Villeveque.

The Battery at this period was also without its trusty B.S.M., Sergeant-Major Beaumont was on leave, and Sergeant Lockley was acting in his stead.

About 11 p.m. on the night of the 17th it began to pour with rain, and most of the men got very wet as there was no shelter. In spite of this, all sections were ready for action soon after midnight.

The attack which was to be launched at 5.20 a.m. on the 18th was a most important one, and had for its objective the capture of the outer defences of the Hindenburg Line. It was to be carried out along the whole front of the Fourth Army, in conjunction with simultaneous attacks by the Third British Army to the north, and the 36th French Corps of the First French Army to the south. The 83rd Brigade, R.G.A., was covering the 6th Division, which comprised the 16th and 71st Brigades. The latter occupied the extreme right of the Fourth Army front and was in touch with the left of the First French Army. The position of the infantry directly in front of us was not entirely satisfactory. Troops of the 11th Essex (71st Brigade) had attacked on the 17th in order to improve the "starting line" for the operations of the next day, but after having taken Trout Copse and, later on, Badger Copse, they encountered considerable opposition round about Holnon village, which changed hands several times. In the early hours of the 18th the situation had not been cleared up, and it was doubtful who held Holnon village.

About 2 a.m. the rain ceased, but at 4 a.m. it commenced again. The detachments on the guns were standing by ready to fire on the first target soon after 5 a.m. At

5.18 a.m. the sections officers were warned from the B.C. Post, " Two minutes to go." Out of the mist and rain one could hear the preparatory order being given to the detachments—" Stand by for salvo " . . . and a few seconds later, " Salvo, fire ! " Once again the crash of the artillery heralded the fact that the British Army was at the throat of the enemy. All guns continued firing at an intense rate. Our fire was directed entirely against hostile batteries, and seems to have been accurate as the reply of the Bosche was not very effective. All sections, however, experienced some shelling. The Right Section, under Lieutenant Allen, got most of this and were lucky in the small number of casualties they had. Unfortunately Lieutenant T. R. Wood, who was commanding the Centre Section, was hit by a splinter which passed right through his arm, and he had in consequence to go to hospital. Lieutenant Curtis carried on as Section Commander. The Left Section, under Lieutenant Hobbs, had several gas shells burst near the guns and the detachments worked for nearly an hour in gas masks. Altogether the Battery fired 404 rounds.

The attack on the Brigade front can scarcely be said to have been successful. When the troops of the 71st Infantry Brigade moved forward at zero the ground was sodden and the progress slow. Considerable machine-gun fire was encountered, especially from Selency, the Quadrilateral and Fresnoy-le-Petit, and the French on the right were also held up. The struggle for Holnon village continued, but the situation became even more obscure. The 16th Brigade (on the left of the 71st Brigade) also met with considerable opposition, but by 8.40 a.m. it had occupied Fresnoy-le-Petit. Later on, however, it was compelled to withdraw from the village. Further north better progress was made, the Australian Corps doing exceptionally well.

At 3.30 p.m. the enemy launched several determined counter-attacks north of Fresnoy-le-Petit. These attacks were held up, but round about the village itself the situation became very involved. Fighting was also renewed round Holnon village and Selency, and with the French on our right in some difficulty the operations immediately in front of the 83rd Brigade R.G.A. became of a defensive rather than an offensive nature. At 6.55 p.m. the Battery was ordered to fire on S.O.S. lines, and the night programme included both S.O.S. and counter-battery targets, in case the enemy should again counter-attack.

In addition to losing the valuable services of Lieutenant T. R. Wood, the Battery suffered five other casualties on September 18th. Two signallers, Gunner J. Brodie (who was on the O.P. line) and Gunner H. Ibbotson were wounded, as were also Gunners J. Kingdon and E. Hassell. Gunner V. Dickerson was killed. Poor Dickerson was very unlucky. He and Hassell were marching up to the position from the billets at Villeveque with the detachments which were to relieve those on the guns. A shell burst just in the rear of the party, killing Gunner Dickerson and wounding Gunner Hassell rather badly. Dickerson belonged to the Left Section. He had done excellent work with the Battery and his Section Commander thought very highly of him.

As was to be expected, the Battery came in for a good deal of shelling during the next few days. The operations of the 18th had disclosed to the enemy the strength of artillery concentrated on the western edge of Holnon and St. Quentin Woods, and the result was that the 83rd Brigade area was subjected to an almost continuous bombardment. The infantry in front of us endeavoured to clear up the situation, but when the 6th Division attacked with the 71st and 16th Brigades on the 19th in the vicinity of the Quadrilateral and at Fresnoy-le-Petit, the opposition encountered was even greater than on the 18th, and no progress was made. Similar unsuccessful attacks were made by the French on the right in the vicinity of Manchester Hill and Round Hill. During the night of the 19th, however, the troops of the 6th Division finally gained Holnon Village, the possession of which had been so fiercely disputed during the last three days. Colonel Curteis, our Brigade Commander, did his utmost to give the infantry all the assistance possible. The firing done during the day of the 19th illustrates that the Battery's guns were anything but idle.

Here is our programme :

N.F. Call : M 24 d 3.7.
N.F. Call : N 31 a 5.6.   } Morning.
Concentration (all guns) N 21 c 20.75

Concentration at 12.30 p.m., 2 p.m. and 3 p.m. (all guns), one round per two minutes for ten minutes on M 24 d 3.7.

Concentration at 12.15 p.m., 2.30 p.m. and 3.30 p.m. (all guns) one round per two minutes for ten minutes on M 5 b 6.7.

Concentration at 12.45 p.m., 1.15 p.m. and 4 p.m. (all

guns) one round per two minutes for ten minutes on G 35 c 35.25.

Attempted Registration on M 18 c 73.80 (apparently difficult to observe as rounds were unobserved).

Successful Registration on M 22 a 9.4.—Fifteen rounds at 4.50 p.m.

The Battery suffered no casualties on the 19th. Lieutenant Hobbs received a slight flesh wound but was able to remain at duty.

On the 20th the enemy endeavoured to wipe the Battery out by a destructive shoot directed by one of his aeroplanes. The following is the official report concerning this which was furnished to Brigade :—

"A shoot, seemingly intended to be destructive, was carried out on the Battery this morning. The sound bearing of the enemy battery appeared to be 85° G. Fire commenced with single gun ranging about 9.20 a.m. An enemy aeroplane was over the Battery from that hour until 10.15 a.m. ranging the enemy guns. Our wireless received his observations which are annexed. After 9.42 there were bursts of gun fire of about ten rounds every four minutes until 10.20. The fire then ceased, but recommenced at 10.40, and continued until 11.0. At 11.15 thirty rounds were fired at five seconds interval, and after that, bursts of gun fire at intervals of five minutes. Firing ceased about midday. The Centre Section (Nos. 3 and 4 guns) appeared to be the objective, but some rounds burst in the vicinity of the Left Section (Nos. 5 and 6 guns). Generally he was plus of the guns and just short of the B.C. post, but of the thirty rounds at 11.15 a.m., several fell in or near the pits of the Centre Section. Before this, the detachments had been cleared from these two guns. Altogether about 200 rounds were fired."

It remains to say that there were no casualties and there was no actual damage to the guns. A small fire was caused in one of the pits of the Centre Section and fourteen rounds of shell, forty fuzes, 340 tubes and seventy-one charges were destroyed. A certain amount of damage was also done to the gun stores, and a number of casualties were caused amongst the personnel of neighbouring batteries of the Brigade. The wireless of 284 S.B., which was in a trench quite close to our B.C. post, was smashed in and the operator and another man severely wounded.

On the morning of the 21st, Lieutenant Allen went on leave. This made the shortage of officers acute. The Major had only three officers left to carry on at the position—Lieutenants Curtis, Hobbs and Gill.

It was not possible to give orders directly from the B.C. post, everything having to be passed by phone to the sections. This meant some very hard work for the signallers, who, besides having to man the sections' phones, had also to be constantly repairing the lines between the B.C. post and the guns which were cut by enemy shell fire with monotonous regularity. To meet all these needs, Lieutenant Curtis, O/C signals, had to keep five men permanently on duty in the Battery, and by day, two more had to be employed with the wireless. Others were on duty under Brigade orders on the O.P. lines, so altogether the signallers were having a rough time. The wireless expert, Second Air Mechanic Hardy, also did excellent work at his post. He made use of a small cellar, which gave some cover, but it was not by any means shell proof.

The 21st was a less strenuous day. The Battery received its fair share of attention from the Bosche, but towards evening things became quiet. Since the 17th every officer had been on duty practically continuously. Major Heath realised that this state of things could not go on indefinitely, and encouraged by the apparent calm suggested that he and two of the three subalterns should make a "pyjama" night of it. This was hailed as a particularly sound idea, and accordingly the Major and Lieutenants Curtis and Gill, after having satisfied the inner man, proceeded to enjoy a well-earned rest. As events turned out, they were most unfortunate in their choice of nights, for the Hun was preparing a very determined effort to rid himself, once and for all, of "135" and the other batteries in the Brigade.

Lieutenant Hobbs took over duty in the B.C. post about 9 p.m., where he found Bombardier Mackenzie, the B.C.A. About 11.10, the enemy started shelling the position with a H.V. gun. The rounds, which were well plus of the guns, were bursting just round the B.C. post trench. A momentary silence was broken by moans quite near, and emerging from the B.C. post, Lieutenant Hobbs almost fell over Fitter Gunner F. Hopkins, who had been badly wounded in the legs. Fortunately he had been using a stretcher to sleep on, and in a very few minutes two other gunners, who had come to the rescue, carried him off to the dressing station. This was a bad start; Hopkins was the Battery "Tiffy," and was a splendid man at his job. However, within half an hour, the enemy's shelling ceased and comparative quiet reigned until about 3 a.m., when a concentrated bombardment commenced on the valley from 8-inch, 5·9-inch and 4·2-inch howitzers and 10-c.m. and 77-m.m. guns. The whole of the Brigade area was under fire, and shells were bursting simultaneously at a most alarming rate. The officer seized the phone, but, as he anticipated, the lines were all down. The noise was terrific, but there was little that could be done. Communication with Brigade was cut off and, even if it were possible to re-establish it, there was no chance of the lines remaining intact for even a few minutes. Bombardier Wickenden and another signaller managed to reach the B.C. post. The former very bravely asked for orders. The officer told him there were none, but that he had better stand by in the B.C. post. The heavy shelling continued: to those in the B.C. post it appeared that all sections were being strafed equally badly, and it seemed certain that a round must sooner or later find its way through the slender cover of the Post itself. About 4 a.m. most of the men of the Centre Section, finding the place where they had taken refuge too warm, made a rush for the B.C. post. They fell into it one after another until the little place was crowded. They presented a sorry spectacle, and several of them seemed to be suffering from the effects of gas poisoning. The officer suggested that they should remain in the Post, but pointed out that it was only splinter proof, and that it might, perhaps, be more advisable for them to endeavour to get out of the shelled area. Just then a shell, bursting a few yards short of the trench, clouded the place with dust, and a few seconds later another, exploding about two yards to the right, put out the candle and shook the whole place to such an extent that it took the occupants some seconds to discover whether they were still in possession of their arms and legs. Having decided this question in the affirmative, Sergeant Marsh's men decided to use the latter forthwith, and dashing out of the B.C. post, were fortunate in reaching a spot where the shelling was less severe. At 5 a.m. the bombardment was continuing with unabated violence. The immediate vicinity of the B.C. post was being cut up so badly that Lieutenant Hobbs suggested to the B.C.A. that if he thought it safer to clear out to a flank there was no reason why he should not do so. Bombardier Mackenzie, who had behaved with admirable coolness throughout, replied: "If you are remaining here, sir, I shall stay with you." About 5.30 a.m. it began to get light, but the shelling did not slacken until about 6.30. The officer then went out to have a look at the damage. One of the guns in the quarry had received a direct hit; the others had escaped serious injury, but the Left Section guns had been splintered somewhat. A considerable amount of ammunition and some stores had been destroyed, and the Centre Section pits were smouldering. Returning to the B.C. post Lieutenant Hobbs met the Major looking very grotesque in British warm, pyjamas and gum boots, and together they went to the B.C. post of 116 Heavy Battery, which, by this time, had got a wire through to Brigade. Bombardier Wickenden had already been at work on our lines for some time, but they were cut so badly that it was some hours before direct communication with Brigade was re-established.

To complete the record of events it is necessary to say something of those of the Battery who were not actually on duty. They fared almost as badly. The following is a verbatim extract from Major Heath's diary:

> "When the show started I was asleep in my 'dug-out,' which would not have stopped a direct hit from anything. I remained there for some time hoping that it was just one of the ordinary concentrations that we were by now getting used to, but as it continued, I put on a British warm and gum boots and doubled along the sunken road northwards for about fifty yards. I crouched in a hole for some time expecting to be blown up any minute, as rounds kept bursting very near—several within a few yards, and one almost next to me. My servant then came running along and I learnt from him that the others were still in their shacks in the sunken road. I went back and routed them all out, telling them to come away to a safer place. Gill had got up and put his breeches on, apparently preferring to make his appearance in the next world in these, but Curtis, who shared his billet, was still in bed! The signallers and servants were also in their dug-outs. I should, I suppose, have gone down to the Battery, but it was really impossible to get there, and I could have

done no good. I took the party through the wood north of the billets, and then left them, telling Curtis to take them away out of the area until the shelling ceased. There was no slackening until well after daylight. I then went down to the Battery and found Hobbs at the B.C. post, where he had remained throughout. Together we went to the B.C. post of 116 Heavy Battery, whose position had not suffered quite so severely, and reported the affair to Brigade H.Q."

Our casualties were surprisingly slight. Sergeant Anderson and Gunners Hepworth, Spooner and Fenton were wounded, and Lance-Bombardier Sexton (one of the old hands who had come out to France with the Battery) and Gunners Lawson, Kinder, Overton and Swindley were admitted to hospital gassed. The detachments on duty in the Right Section for the most part took cover in a railway cutting to the right of their guns; while the Left Section took refuge in the slit-trenches they had constructed and which seem to have served them admirably. The detachments of the Centre Section have already been referred to.

Shelling of the valley continued at intervals throughout the morning. The day before, the Major had given orders for the whole Battery, including the office staff, to leave the billet position at Villeveque and come up to live at the fighting position. They duly arrived in the afternoon of the 22nd, during another very unpleasant concentration from the Bosche. Corporal Hinchcliffe, our much respected "Registrar, Accountant and Auditor General," was wounded while arriving with the Battery records. As it seemed certain that the introduction of more men into the area would mean an increase in casualties, Major Heath decided to retain the old billet position, and accordingly the party was sent back.

About 4 p.m. Colonel Curteis spoke to the B.C. post. He said he was sick of reading the daily reports recording Hun shelling, and it was quite time that something was done to stop it. He proposed sending immediately to all batteries in the Brigade certain known locations of enemy batteries, with instructions that as soon as the Bosche opened fire it was to be returned. Shortly after, a dispatch-rider arrived with the locations of five hostile batteries. These targets were allotted to the sections with orders that the guns, when not on S.O.S. lines, were to remain layed on them, and in the event of the enemy opening fire, all guns were to answer immediately without further orders from the B.C. post. Arrangements were made for corrections consequent on the latest " Meteor " wire being passed on to the guns. The idea was taken up very keenly by the detachments, and the batteries of the Brigade were so near to each other that one or two rounds put over by the enemy were always sufficient to produce a most generous acknowledgment from practically every available gun in the Brigade.

Whatever the cause, after the 22nd, the Bosche was not nearly so troublesome, but we were all pleased when it became known that we were shortly to move to another position.

On the 23rd, the Major met the Colonel and the other Battery Commanders at the Quarries east of Vermand, on the Vermand—St. Quentin road, with a view to selecting the new position. The requirements were that it should be possible for the guns to enfilade the Canal west and north of Bellenglise, which at that point formed the chief obstacle in the famous Hindenburg Line. The Major finally decided on a position at the north-western edge of the St. Quentin Wood where it meets the Vermand—St. Quentin road.

The Battery was destined to take part in one more operation before leaving the ill-fated position in front of Attilly. It had been agreed between Marshal Foch and Sir Douglas Haig that a general attack on the Hindenburg Line was likely to meet with success, providing it could be made immediately. Four convergent and simultaneous offensives were to be launched by the Allies ; one by the Americans west of the Meuse in the direction of Mezières ; the second by the French, west of the Argonne ; the third by the British on the St. Quentin—Cambrai front, in the direction of Maubeuge ; and the fourth by the Belgian and Allied forces in Flanders. The success of this combined offensive rested entirely on the taking of the Hindenburg Line by the British Armies. The outer defences had already to a great extent been overcome by operations since September 18th, but the position on the extreme right of the British line directly in front of the Battery was still unsatisfactory. With a view to improving the situation prior to the general attack which had been fixed to take place on the 29th, a local attack was arranged for

The Battery Position behind St. Quentin and Holnon Woods, September, 1918.
From a Water Colour Drawing by Lieutenant C. R. Hurle Hobbs.

September 24th. It was launched at 5 a.m. The Battery supported this with its five remaining guns, firing in all 450 rounds. In spite of stubborn resistance on the part of the enemy the attack was successful, and although all objectives were not secured on the opening day, the progress made rendered the strong points which the enemy continued to defend, untenable; and by maintaining pressure on September 25th and 26th, our infantry finally secured the maze of trenches known as the Quadrilateral, and the French captured Francilly-Selency and Manchester Hill.

The Battery had already begun work on the new position. Lieutenant Gill with a working party had started on the pits on the 23rd, and on the night of the 24th the Left Section, under Lieutenant Hobbs, moved to the new position. The Centre Section and the remaining gun of the Right Section still remained at the old position and (in order to deceive the Hun as to our movements) fired 104 rounds on the morning of the 25th. All guns were finally pulled out of action on the night of September 25th.

In closing this chapter of the Holnon position a word must be said in praise of all ranks who, during ten days, had been subjected to practically a continuous bombardment in a position bare of cover. During this period the men worked bravely and cheerfully, and each one may feel justly proud of the part he played. There is a passage in Major Heath's diary which we think should be included here.

> " The Germans shelled the valley almost continuously. They had a most annoying way of putting sudden concentrations of many guns down on various spots without warning. After some time these tended to have a very nerve-shattering effect, as one never knew when they were coming. During this trying time I was very thankful to have the cheerful support of Curtis, Hobbs and Gill, none of whom seemed to get rattled at anything that happened, and all showed a very fine example to the men. Allen went on leave on the 21st and so missed the worst period, but he too was, as usual, a great help while there. They were all willing to laugh at anything that happened and regard it as a joke. If it had not been for this I should have found it very hard to carry on. The N.C.O.'s and men also behaved splendidly, and

in spite of the rough time they were experiencing I never heard a single grouse."

As has been already mentioned, Lieutenant Jones was engaged entirely on O.P. duty. This occupied him every day and most nights. His experience during the ten days was a most trying one, but he stuck to his job and did splendid work.

CHAPTER XIV

The Breaking of the Hindenburg Line

[September 25th to 29th, 1918]

The new position had a bad reputation for "concentrations." It was well in front of all other batteries of the Brigade, and during the time Lieutenant Gill was there with his working party the place was shelled badly. As it turned out, however, our experience was a happy one. There was a certain amount of material about which was used in the construction of shelters for the gun detachments and an excellent B.C. post. The sections were kept as far apart as possible. On the north of the Vermand—St. Quentin road, about two hundred yards N.E. of the western corner of St. Quentin Wood, there was a quarry which gave admirable cover for the two guns of the Centre Section. Its one drawback was its dangerous proximity to a road which was almost certain to receive a certain amount of bombing and shelling. About two hundred yards to the rear of the Centre Section, and also on the north of the road, a place was found for the remaining gun of the Right Section. This was quite in the open and could probably be seen from at least one enemy kite balloon. The Left Section guns were just inside the western edge of the wood about three hundred yards south of the road.

The guns were got into position on the night of September 25th. There was no interference from the enemy's artillery, but his planes did a considerable amount of bombing in the neighbourhood of the position. One bomb exploded about ten yards from one of the guns of the Left Section, but fortunately no one was hurt. Another which was dropped from the same plane a few seconds later set fire to some of the ammunition of the Centre Section and caused a blaze for a short time.

The Major decided to have all the personnel at the new

position, and so, when the move had been completed, the rear billet at Villeveque was finally dispensed with.

The great affair on hand was the smashing of the Hindenburg Line. In order to render this possible, it was recognised that a heavy preliminary bombardment would be necessary. It was useless to rely on the element of surprise which had made the attack of August 8th so successful. On that occasion the enemy's defences were of the ordinary trench character, but the Hindenburg Line on which so much scientific labour had been expended since the end of 1916, presented the strongest fortified line which any attacking troops had ever attempted to force. The Fourth Army were to attack on a front of about twelve miles, from Selency to Vendhuile. The attack of the IX Corps was to be launched on the southern part of the Army front and was to extend from Selency on the extreme right to somewhere in the neighbourhood of Buisson Gaulaine Farm, a distance of about 10,000 yards. On this part of the front the enemy had made use of the St. Quentin Canal to protect the main line of his defence which was on the eastern bank, and along the whole length of the canal there were concrete structures for harbouring machine guns, and numerous belts of wire. The canal contained some depth of water round about Bellenglise, where it had been dammed, but away to the south of the village the bed was almost dry.

The following are the orders which were issued by General Head-quarters regulating the attack :

"The 1st Army will attack on Z day with a view to capturing the heights of Bourlon Wood in the first instance. It will then push forward and secure its left on the Sensée River and operate so as to protect the left of the 3rd Army.

"The 3rd Army will operate in the direction of the general line Le Cateau—Solesmes. It will attack on 'Z' day in conjunction with the 1st Army, and will press forward to secure the passages of the Canal de l'Escaut, so as to be in a position to co-operate closely with the 4th Army on 'Z + 2 day.' The 3rd Army will assist the 4th Army with counter battery work on the enemy's guns in the region La Terrière—Villers Outréaux.

"The 4th Army, protected on its right flank by the 1st French Army, will deliver the main attack against the enemy's defences from Le Tronquoy to Le Catelet, both inclusive, operating in the direction of the general line, Bohain—Busigny. The bombardment will commence on 'Z' day and the assault will be delivered on 'Z + 2 day.'"

Later it was notified that "Z" day would be September 27th, on which day it will be noted the bombardment by the Fourth Army was to begin. The actual assault, however, on the Fourth Army front was not to be launched until September 29th—" Z + 2 day."

" Zero " hour on " Z + 2 day " was fixed for 5.50 a.m., and the 48-hour bombardment was to commence on September 27th at 6 a.m.

The object of this preliminary work by the artillery was, first and foremost, to destroy as far as possible the strong defences of the enemy. There were miles of wire which had to be cut in order to facilitate the movements of the infantry. This task was allotted to 4·5-inch and 6-inch howitzers. The neutralisation of enemy batteries was also undertaken and his communications harassed unceasingly. In addition, all his known strong-points were subjected to heavy concentrations throughout the forty-eight hours. At 5.50 a.m. on September 29th the actual attack was launched. The southern flank of the IX Corps, which our Brigade was supporting, advanced to the attack, the 1st Division going forward to secure the right flank of the 46th Division, which advanced to the storming of the strong line of the canal and the capture of Bellenglise. There was a dense mist which was soon intensified by the smoke of the barrage, but the canal was reached in good time and was crossed just north-west of Bellenglise. Bellenglise itself was then taken, and the tunnel entrances in the village captured, together with a large number of prisoners. The resistance of the enemy, which had been moderately strong when the attack was first launched, was soon overcome, and once the line of the canal was crossed the efforts of the enemy to rally and present organised resistance were spasmodic only, and were never such as could withstand the victorious onrush of our gallant troops.

The part which the Battery had the honour to play in the splendid achievement of September 29th was necessarily not so dramatic as the wonderful doings of the infantry, but entailed work of a very heavy and sustained nature. One thousand two hundred and fifty rounds were fired during the preliminary bombardment, and on the day of the attack 857 rounds were fired between 5.50 a.m. and 2.28 p.m. This means that in sixty-two and a half hours 2,107 rounds of H.E. shell, approximating in weight to nearly 200 tons, were fired by the five howitzers of the Battery.

The Fourth Army had available for the attack 1,044 guns served by the R.F.A. and 593 guns served by Heavy and Siege batteries. The actual expenditure of ammunition on September 27th, 28th and 29th by these guns was as follows:

Guns.		Howitzers.	
13-pounder - -	11,167	4·5-inch - -	101,356
18-pounder - -	379,960	6-inch - - -	128,211
60-pounder - -	44,726	8-inch - - -	19,233
6-inch - - -	4,530	9·2-inch - -	13,217
12-inch - - -	73	12-inch - - -	1,278
14-inch - - -	48		
	440,504		263,295

703,799

These figures prove conclusively that the Hun must have had anything but a good time, and one certain effect of the bombardment was the shattering of the enemy's morale. It is equally certain, from the evidence of prisoners captured during the attack, that the troops manning his front lines had been without food during the two days of the preliminary bombardment, the harassing fire on his communications rendering all means of transport impossible.

The reply of the enemy artillery during the attack was very weak, and the Battery did not suffer a single casualty. By the afternoon most of the enemy guns which might have worried us had either been captured or withdrawn. The enemy was once more in full retreat, and our cavalry were going up so as to harass him still further. It was known that there were no defences of a very strong nature behind the formidable line which had just been broken, and the enthusiasm of the troops was so great that the very atmosphere seemed impregnated with victory.

The gunners began to speculate as to what their next job would be. It was obviously impossible to charge into a retreating enemy with 8-inch howitzers, but experience had taught them the improbability of their being allowed to remain idle for long.

The Battery was still very short of officers, and allotments of leave had on two occasions to be withheld. On September 27th Captain Hickson had returned, and this made it possible to spare Lieutenant Gill, who proceeded on leave the next day. Lieutenant Noakes returned on the 30th, and on the following day Lieutenant Hobbs started off for Boulogne.

On the afternoon of September 29th the 6-inch and 60-pounder batteries of the Brigade advanced by stages to the valley west of Joncourt, and the Brigade H.Q. was moved up to Harry Copse (about a mile north of Bellenglise). Orders came through that 135 S.B. and 69 S.B. (the 9·2-inch battery) were to be attached to the 14th Brigade, R.G.A., and left behind for the time being, as the roads were too crowded to allow of the advancing of heavy guns. The Major visited the 83rd Brigade H.Q. occasionally, but the Colonel could only say that he would have us up as soon as he was allowed to.

In the meantime all the gun platforms were taken up and three caterpillars (which were all that were available at the time) stood by in anticipation of orders to advance.

The platforms, carriers and many other stores were beginning to get rather the worse for wear, and some time was spent in overhauling and making good the defective parts. The Signallers, under Lieutenant Curtis, took advantage of the spare time and managed to "scrounge" large supplies of telephone wires which other batteries, advancing hurriedly, had failed to reel in.

CHAPTER XV

MAGNY-LA-FOSSE TO BOHAIN

[OCTOBER, 1918]

About 6.45 p.m. on October 3rd orders came from the 83rd Brigade H.Q. for Major Heath to report to the Colonel. The Major reached Brigade about 7.30 p.m. and received instructions to reconnoitre a position between Magny-la-Fosse and the Bellenglise—Joncourt road, and to move the Battery up that night. It was quite dark before the Major reached the area in which he was to select the new Battery position. After taking a rapid survey of the country he decided that, as there was no cover of any sort, the only thing necessary was to select a position as far distant from the road as was compatible with easy access. Having settled on the approximate positions for the guns, the Major hastened to return to the Battery. The journey back, however, was a tedious affair owing to the crowded state of the roads. The cavalry which had been in action were returning, and transport of every description was coming up against them. To add to the confusion, German planes started bombing all along the road. At one stage, a bomb landed in the midst of a batch of Hun prisoners, who sent up frantic wailings, screaming " Kamerad, liebe kamerad ! "

The Major finally reached the old position at 10.30 p.m., and at 11 p.m. the three guns for which caterpillars were available moved off from St. Quentin Wood. The usual digging party went on in advance. By the route which the Battery had to take (*via* Vermand), the distance to the new position was approximately ten miles. In spite of this, the guns were in action on their Vickers platforms by 8 a.m. on the next day. A move of such rapidity could not have been effected had not the detachments worked with extraordinary energy. Shelling was continuous to the right of the position throughout the night and numerous splinters came along, but fortunately there were no casualties. On the evening of October 4th, the other two guns came up and were got into position. The five guns were in line just east of the road running north from Magny-la-Fosse, and occupied a frontage of about 250 yards. It was possible for lorries to come in from the road and bring ammunition right up to the guns.

The advance of our infantry had been temporarily held up along the line Mont Brehain—east of Sequehart—east of St. Quentin. Immediately in front of the Battery the enemy held the high ground south and east of Mont Brehain. His defences were no longer of a very formidable nature, and comprised hastily constructed trenches and such obstacles as the nature of the country provided.

On October 5th Lieutenant Allen returned from leave and was greeted with the news that he had been posted as Captain to 284 Siege Battery. It is true to say that any joy which he may have felt at his promotion was completely nullified by his regret at leaving the Battery. He was the last of the officers who had come out with the Battery in 1916, and the personnel were devotedly attached to him. He had always been cheerful and courageous under difficulties, and had played for his side with commendable loyalty. Our only consolation was, that as he was joining Major Phillips, he would still, so to speak, be one of the family. The same night Second Lieutenant Mears joined the Battery from England.

Early in the morning of October 6th enemy planes, which had continued to worry us nightly, bombed the Battery rather badly. One explosion was quite close to the B.C. post where Lieutenant Jones and Bombardier Mackenzie were on duty. It set fire to the tarpaulin and supports, and a lot of the Battery papers, including records of registration, calibration, etc., were burnt. The fighting map was also destroyed. Another bomb dropped close to No. 2 gun, killing Gunner Woolley and wounding Gunner J. Smith, who were sleeping quite near to the gun. Woolley was a fine sample of a gunner—a big, healthy fellow, who had done splendid work in his Section. Gunner Smith was also a great loss, as he was one of the best workers in his detachment and possessed no little skill in dealing with the equipment. The Battery lost two other good men on this date—Gunners Doughty and Pearson, both of whom were wounded.

On October 8th, the attack of the IX Corps was resumed in conjunction with the French on its right and the II American Corps on its left. The attack which was launched under cover of a heavy artillery fire was very successful. Mannequin Hill, Doon Hill and Beauregard Farm were captured, and later, the village of Mericourt fell to the 16th Brigade. The Battery supported this attack with the usual counter-battery fire. We had only four guns in action, as the I.O.M. had condemned one of the pieces the day before. Lieutenant Noakes acted as Brigade F.O.O. during the attack, and had with him Bombardier Crumpling and another signaller. By 8 a.m. the Battery was almost out of range. Additional targets were, however, sent in at intervals by Brigade, and we continued firing at very long range until 3.30 p.m., when we finished with a concentration on L'Esperance. About 11 a.m. the Major had gone forward to find Lieutenant Noakes with a view to establishing an O.P. from which to observe our distant fire. Having borrowed one of the motor-bikes he made for Doon Hill, and found that from there a fine view could be obtained. He failed to find Lieutenant Noakes, however, and decided to go back to the O.P. just north of Presselles where there was a Brigade telephone exchange. Having arrived in the vicinity of the exchange he left the motor-cycle on the roadside and made across country for about 200 yards. He was informed at the exchange that Lieutenant Noakes and his party had been there but had gone forward in the direction of Doon Hill. The Major decided to follow them up, but on reaching the road again discovered that the motor-bike had been "found" by some other gentleman, who seems to have thought it dangerous to leave it so exposed. The Major was therefore forced to foot it to Doon Hill, and by walking along the wire which Lieutenant Noakes had laid from the exchange he finally came up with the party.

Lieutenant Noakes and his party spent the night at Doon Hill on Brigade O.P. duty. The Major, on his way back to the Battery, managed to borrow a car from Major Phillips of 284 S.B., who had now advanced to Mont Brehain. As soon as he arrived at the Battery he was handed orders from Brigade to move up that night to Ramicourt.

Leaving Captain Hickson to send on a working party and to bring up the guns later, the Major and Lieutenant

Jones hurried off in the borrowed car to select a position. They arrived at Ramicourt at 11 p.m., and finally found suitable places for the four guns at the south-western edge of the village. Two were under cover of some trees and two were in the open. The working party under Lieutenant Mears were a long time getting to the position as they were delayed on the road, but finally arrived about 1 a.m. The guns turned up later with the platforms, and the Battery was in action soon after midday on the 9th.

Very little firing was done from the new position, and on October 11th we were again out of range. The platforms were taken up and preparations made for the next move forward.

On October 12th the Major was ordered to report to the IX Corps H.A. Headquarters to meet Colonel Curteis and receive orders. He was instructed to proceed to Bohain and to select a position just north of the town in an area of which he was given the co-ordinates. The Battery were to move up that night. The Major sent back orders to the Battery to get on to the road, arranging to meet them at a point on the Brancourt—Bohain road at 2.30 in the afternoon. This did not leave him much time, as he had to select his position and report to Brigade H.Q. (which were then about two miles north-west of Bohain), before occupying it. He started off from Corps H.Q. by motor-cycle, but before he had covered more than 500 yards something went wrong with the engine, which refused all treatment which the Major endeavoured to administer. With many muttered curses the cycle was finally consigned to a ditch by the side of the road, and having possessed himself of the chain, the Major started off again on foot. An attempt made later in the day to recover the bike proved abortive. It was never seen by the Battery again. Possibly it found an " owner " who was more patient with its defects and had more time to attend to its ailments. This was the second motor-cycle which the Major lost in three days!

The town of Bohain had only just been taken by us and was practically intact. There were several thousands of French inhabitants who had remained there throughout the German occupation. These good people produced flags as if by magic and gave the British troops a rousing welcome when the town was entered. The recovery of these inhabited towns and villages provided perhaps the most stirring incidents of the great advance. Here the British Tommy saw the practical results of his years of fighting. Can it be wondered that, having reached that stage, no efforts of the enemy would have sufficed to stay the enthusiastic onslaught of the Allied Armies ?

The Major selected a position for the Battery in a field about 700 yards north of the town and just east of the road to Becquigny. Having reported to Brigade and borrowed a car, he went back in search of the Battery and found them at the place he had arranged. The guns were pulled in that night without incident.

During the next few days a certain amount of firing was done on targets sent through by Brigade. The Battery was living in a most luxurious style, being billeted in the town and having a daily supply of green vegetables from the ample provision made by the Bosche, who had put large areas of land under cultivation and forced practically the whole of the female population to work on the soil.

On October 15th the Major reconnoitred for a new O.P.: the one we had been using was on the top of a hill about 1,000 yards north of the battery position, and was too far distant from the Hun to afford any specially exciting observation. Major Phillips, whose battery was near Becquigny, was using an O.P. in the Bois de Busigny, and it was thither that the Major directed his steps. He found Major Phillips bombarding the front line German trench, and the Huns could be plainly seen dodging about to avoid the shells. The O.P. was a good one, but was a long way from the Battery position. However, Lieutenant Curtis had a good supply of wire, and the next day a line was laid from the Battery to the new O.P. and the guns registered successfully on a point in the neighbourhood of La Vallée Mulâtre.

The same day operation orders were received for an attack which was to be launched on the morrow at 5.20 a.m. The chief obstacle to our advance was provided by the River Selle, and the object of the attack was to capture the whole country lying between the Selle and the Sambre and Oise Canal. The attack was to be made by the IX Corps, the II American Corps, and the XIII Corps, and the objectives given were as follows :

First Objective.—Andigny-les-Fermes — Molain — St. Martin-Rivere and St. Souplet.

Second Objective.—La Vallée Mulâtre—the farms Jonc de Mer and La Roux, and the town of Le Cateau (an advance to an average depth of 1,750 yards beyond the first objective).

Third Objective.—A further advance of some 3,000 yards including the capture of Wassigny, Mazinghien and Basuel.

Fourth Objective.—The Sambre and Oise Canal between La Laurette and Catillon.

As on previous occasions, the First French Army on the right of the Corps were to advance simultaneously and protect our southern flank.

After having made final preparations for the attack the Major turned in at about 10.30 p.m. He seems to have had his peace of mind somewhat disturbed during the night, as will be shown from the following extract which is taken from his diary:

"I could not have slept long when my phone started buzzing. I found that the Brigade Adjutant was at the other end of the wire. I at once foresaw trouble when he began, 'You registered on a point in La Vallée Mulâtre to-day, didn't you?' I agreed that we did. 'What O.P. did you observe from?' This rather staggered me, but I admitted that we had used one in the Bois de Busigny. 'What line did you use?' Again I stuck boldly to the truth and said that we had laid one ourselves. 'Well, the 6-inch batteries will probably have to advance to-morrow, so will you please send out a party at once and reel in your line and hand it over to 284 S.B. at Becquigny to-night—Good-bye.' My feelings and language at this can be better imagined than expressed. The wire my signallers had unofficially scrounged during the past weeks in order to build up a reserve for our own purposes was to be thus unfeelingly snatched from us and three men were to be sent out to spend a perfectly rotten night in undoing the work of laying the line which had been carried out earlier in the day. However, it was an order, and in spite of my private feelings I appreciated that it was necessary, as the Brigade at the time was very short of telephone wire. A party was detailed for the work and the wire was duly handed over to 284 S.B. I expect Sergeant Allan, their Signals N.C.O. (late of '135') laughed when he got it."

The attack the next morning was a complete success.

It was launched in a dense mist. By 7.30 a.m. the 46th Division on the extreme right of the IX Corps front had completed the capture of its first objectives, and by 10.30 a.m. the 6th Division (on the left of the 46th) had achieved a similar success. Farther north the XIII Corps, after a splendid attack by the South African Brigade, completed the capture of Le Cateau.

The Battery supported the attack, firing 290 rounds on enemy batteries in the neighbourhood of Wassigny and La Valleé Mulâtre. By 11.22 a.m. we were out of range.

As a result of the day's fighting the first objective along the whole front of the three Corps that attacked had been taken. The French on our right had also met with considerable success. Orders were issued on the night of the 17th for the attack to be continued on the next day.

The 6-inch and 60-pounder batteries of the Brigade advanced with four guns. The remaining Sections of these batteries, together with "69" and "135," were ordered to remain behind at Bohain, and constituted a "Rear Echelon" of the Brigade, of which Major Heath was given the command.

The infantry continued its attack on October 18th. The IX Corps made good progress, capturing Andigny Forest and reaching Wassigny. In conjunction with the II American Corps it captured Ribeauville. The American Corps also did well and took the farms Jonc de Mer and La Roux. The XIII Corps captured Basuel, and after stiff fighting secured the ridge lying between Le Cateau and the Richemont River. The next day the Battle of the Selle came to an end. All objectives had been taken, together with over 5,000 prisoners and sixty guns. The Fourth Army had advanced over five miles on a front of nearly eight miles.

From October 18th to 28th the Battery spent a quiet time out of action at Bohain. The enemy had abandoned his night bombing, but from the 18th to the 20th a 9-inch H.V. gun occasionally shelled Bohain. On the former date Gunner T. Wade was unfortunately wounded and died the same night. He had only been with the Battery for a few weeks, but during that time he had created a very good impression.

On the 19th, Lieutenant Curtis was temporarily attached to Brigade Headquarters as signals officer. It was thought at the time that this might be serious for us, as he knew exactly how much wire we had and we were expecting to be asked to hand some of it over. However, it seems he never forgot that he was still of 135 S.B., and our supply remained intact.

Two new officers joined the Battery while we were at Bohain—Second Lieutenant Phaup and Second Lieutenant Webster. Lieutenant Hobbs returned from leave on October 27th, and the next day Lieutenant T. R. Wood, who it will be remembered was wounded at Attilly, rejoined from hospital.

CHAPTER XVI

RIBEAUVILLE

[NOVEMBER, 1918]

On October 29th the Brigade Commander took Major Heath to a little place called Ecaillon, about half a mile north-east of Ribeauville, where a new battery position was to be selected for another attack, which was to take place within the next few days. The next day the Major, accompanied by Lieutenants Wood and Hobbs, went up to the position with a working party and the digging of the trenches for the platforms was commenced. The Right and Centre Sections were in an orchard on the right of the Ribeauville—Mazinghein road, and about half-way between the two villages. The trees were to serve as camouflage and slit trenches were to be dug to afford protection to the detachments in case of hostile shelling. The Left Section was on the left of the road in a field bare of cover with the exception of a hedge. Emplacements for the guns were chosen quite close up to the hedge so that some cover from view might be obtained.

The enemy was making a determined stand along the bank of the Sambre and Oise canal. His line for the most part ran along the eastern bank of the canal, but to the north of the Battery he occupied the village of Catillon and parts of Ors. Although it may have been the intention of the enemy to carry out a further retirement, it was absolutely essential to him that the passage of the canal should not be made by our troops until he had been able to complete his arrangements for an orderly withdrawal. The following Army Order, addressed to the XVIII German Army by the Crown Prince, supplies conclusive evidence that the enemy intended to maintain the canal line :—

> "The defence of the Canal is of great strategical importance for the Army Group front. I reckon absolutely on the Army holding its new position at all costs."

RIBEAUVILLE.

THE BATTERY'S LAST FIGHTING POSITION.

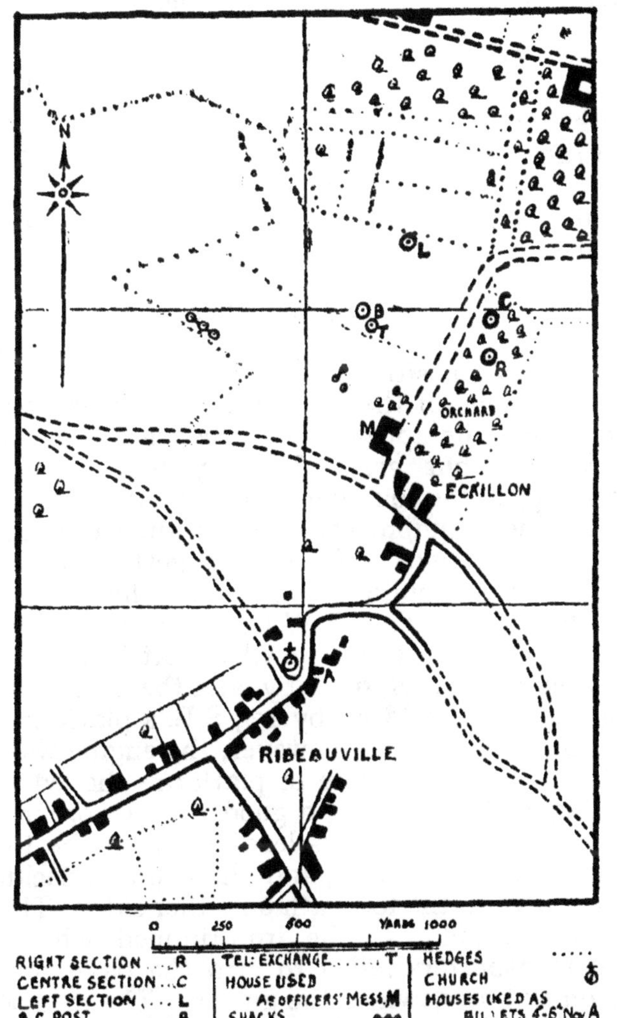

"The reserves at the Army's disposal should be engaged and utilised with a view to this. It must be clearly understood by all Commanding Officers that only a stubborn resistance will induce the enemy to discontinue his attack. Again, I order that the Canal front be strongly reinforced with machine-gun units. I insist upon no further withdrawal being undertaken without my authority.

"(Signed), WILHELM, Crown Prince.

"The above is to be issued down to regiments.

"Signed), BURKNER, Chief of Staff."

Lieutenant Wood and the working party remained at the position on the night of October 30/31st in order to help the unloading of the ammunition supply which was expected to come along. Lieutenants Jones and Hobbs and a party of sixty men paraded at 3.30 a.m. on the morning of October 31st, in order to help in getting the Vickers platforms to the new position. Five F.W.D.'s were to be lent to the Battery for this purpose and were to be at the Bohain position at 5 a.m.

At 7 a.m. none of the F.W.D.'s had arrived, but shortly after, one made its appearance. The other three turned up about 8 a.m., but great difficulty was experienced in limbering-up, as the coupling arrangements on the F.W.D.'s were for 6-inch equipment. It was almost 9 a.m. before the platforms moved off. Before getting clear of the town there was another delay. In the middle of the market-place the leading F.W.D. broke down with engine trouble. The road was so crowded that it was impossible for the other platforms to get by, and the British Army was in danger of being held up by 135 S.B.'s platforms. After half an hour's persuasion, however, the engine was induced to work, and the procession of platforms moved off again, the leading F.W.D. setting a good pace in order to make up for lost time. The roads leading out of the town were constructed of pavé stones, and there was a decided slope from the centre to the footpath on either side. This caused considerable trouble, as the iron-rimmed wheels of the platform transporters failed to grip the pavé surface and insisted on sliding down to the gutter. The men who were riding on the platforms had an exciting time, and troops on the road gazed in astonishment when they saw the platform of No. 3 gun carry down a telegraph post which had presumed to get in its way. Things went well until the village of Vaux Andigny was in sight. It was then that the platform of No. 2 gun quietly but deliberately settled itself down on the road. Only those who have had the misfortune to have to deal with the Vickers 8-inch platform can realise the sinking feeling that one experiences on such an occasion. Lieutenants Jones and Hobbs deliberated, and it was decided that the latter should go on to the position with the four platforms, which were still riding well, and that Lieutenant Jones should bring up the other one as soon as he could get it off the ground. The four platforms eventually reached the position about 1.30 p.m., and about 3.0 p.m. Lieutenant Jones arrived triumphantly with the fifth.

Four guns arrived about 7 p.m. They, too, had been unfortunate in the matter of accidents and the fifth gun was still some way back along the road, its caterpillar having broken down. Lieutenant Beavan had arranged to send one of the other " cats " back for it as soon as one should be free.

The Battery had a very unpleasant time pulling in. It was a wet night and the ground was very sticky. Moreover, the positions which had been chosen for the guns were not easily accessible, and considerable time was taken up in clearing away obstacles which obstructed the entry of the guns. The Hun shelled almost continuously during the whole of the night, and on several occasions the detachments sought cover in the slit-trenches which had fortunately already been dug to a depth of five or six feet. Lieutenants Howell and Beavan, the column officers, were both in the position superintending the work of the caterpillar drivers, which proceeded steadily and calmly in spite of the shelling which was going on all round. Second Lieutenant Webster, who had recently joined us and was under fire for the first time, did some good work with a rum jar which he tucked under one arm while going from section to section issuing, it is feared, rather more than the Army ration. It is extraordinary what a beneficial effect a tot of rum has under such conditions, and Lieutenant Webster's efforts were certainly much appreciated. Lieutenant Beavan proved his best customer, but there were others who similarly felt it incumbent on them to patronise the jar more than once.

About midnight the enemy put over a sharp concentration of 4·2's and frightened us into our slit-trenches. Unfortunately we had a casualty on Number 1 gun. Gunner F. Brace was struck by a splinter while in one of the slit-trenches. It pierced his steel helmet and he died almost immediately. Although he had only joined the Battery a few days before, Gunner Brace was already very much liked and seemed to be a young man of great promise. It was most unfortunate that he should have been knocked out so shortly before the cessation of hostilities.

A little later, Sergeant A. G. Marsh was wounded in the head while superintending the work in D Sub-section. He had joined the Battery as a Corporal with the section from 258 Siege Battery and had proved himself a most efficient No. 1. His detachment had implicit confidence in him. Sergeant Marsh, in charge of his men during a move, provided a splendid example of how things should be done. Scarcely a word was spoken: every man seemed to know his particular job and to work automatically as part of a machine deriving its energy from the Sergeant who would himself work doggedly the whole time.

The Hun had not quite finished with us. Just before midnight Gunner F. Wright was wounded rather badly in the back. He was in considerable pain, and owing to the shelling it was some minutes before he could be got away to a dressing station.

By midnight the Left Section, which had only one gun to see to, had completed their work, and the detachments went off and gave a hand in pulling in one of the guns of the Centre Section before being dismissed for the night. The remainder of the Battery were occupied most of the night in getting the guns into the orchard. The men worked well in spite of the shelling and never sought cover unless ordered to do so. Bombardier Ainsworth did very good work. The gun belonging to D Sub-section gave the most trouble and was not finally put into position until 6 a.m., and then only after all the men of the other sub-sections, who had been dismissed, had been turned out to haul on the drag ropes.

The Battery was now well supplied with officers. The duties were distributed as follows:—

Major Heath—Captain Hickson.

Right Section.—Lieutenant Jones, Lieutenant Phaup.

Centre Section.—Lieutenant T. R. Wood, Lieutenant O. L. Gill.

Left Section.—Lieutenant Hobbs, Lieutenant Webster.

Signallers.—Lieutenant Curtis.

O.P. Duties.—Lieutenant Noakes, Lieutenant Mears.

On November 1st, Major Heath reconnoitred for an O.P.

On the high ground south-west of Catillon, about 150 yards south of the Mazinghein-Catillon road, he found a small trench about five feet deep and twenty feet long. This gave a fairly extensive view of the enemy's position, but the country was so wooded and cut up with hedges that it was difficult to see anything but trees.

The next day a line was laid to this O.P., and on November 3rd the guns were registered and calibrated. After the shoot the Major and Lieutenant Noakes explored the country in order to see if the ground north-west of Catillon provided more favourable observation. They were uncertain as to the position of our front line, and while returning by what seemed to be a short cut, were startled by an excited exclamation from a hedge about a hundred yards behind them. On going back to verify the cause of this alarm they learned that they had passed our front line posts and at the time their attention had been attracted were making direct for the Bosche line!

November 4th witnessed the last prepared attack on the enemy. The objective was the taking of the canal line. In order to effect this difficult task the engineers had been employed for several days previously in devising portable bridges, ferries, etc., by which the troops should be enabled to get to the eastern bank. In addition, most of the troops who were to be entrusted with the launching of the attack were provided with life belts.

Zero hour was 5.45 a.m. There was a thick ground mist when the attack opened, but troops of the 1st, 2nd and 3rd Brigades moved forward to the assault with wonderful energy. The Battery opened fire at Zero with each gun on a different hostile battery. A system was employed by which Brigade gave the same target to several of the batteries with instructions that one gun should be employed by each battery on each of the several targets. This must have had the effect of assuring some accurate fire on the enemy's positions, as any faulty shooting by one battery would most probably be counterbalanced by more accurate fire from other batteries in the Brigade.

From 5.45 to 10 a.m. the five guns in action fired 480 rounds, and later, N.F. and other aeroplane calls were answered which brought the total number of rounds fired up to 762. The enemy replied at intervals during the morning, some of his bursts of fire being rather severe. About 10.30 a.m. several rounds fell just close to a small cottage which was being used as an officers' mess, and one of these actually hit our treasured side-car and so put an end to its existence. A tribute must be paid to this long-suffering piece of mechanism which had endured uncomplainingly some very rough handling by subalterns who were quite unacquainted with the delicacy of its anatomy. It died, so to speak, in harness (if one may be permitted to use that term of an automobile), and there can be no doubt that its end was more honourable than that of being knocked down under the hammer of the Disposal Board.

The troops in front of us had met with splendid success. Having made the crossing of the canal they went forward with great dash. The villages of Catillon, Mezières, La Groise and Fesmy were taken, together with a large number of prisoners and guns.

At 3.12 p.m. the Battery received an N.F. call on a target which was engaged by firing twelve rounds. These were the last rounds which the Battery fired in the war.

As a result of the attack the Sambre and Oise Canal had been crossed from a point some 3,000 yards south of Catillon to Landrecies, and our troops were already some three miles beyond its eastern bank. The days following present the picture of the British Army pressing back a disordered and beaten enemy over the same ground which in 1914 the small handful of British soldiers had so valiantly disputed. When the word to cease fire was passed down on the memorable morning of November 11th, the Allied Armies were more than justified in congratulating one another on the finest victory which has ever been or is ever likely to be chronicled in the world's history.

CHAPTER XVII

After the Armistice

It would be premature to close this record here without some reference to those days which intervened between the signing of the Armistice and the final disbanding of the Battery. It was perhaps natural that the thoughts of every one should turn towards home, and it is certain that the greater part of the Battery imagined that in a few weeks they would be making their adieux to the shores of France. As events turned out, demobilisation took a considerable time.

The Battery were quartered at Wassigny when news of the Armistice came through. No attempt will be made here to describe the joy which every one felt. It was the day we had all longed for, but to such an extent had the war become the only thing in our existence that it seemed hardly credible that we were not to fire again.

The 83rd Brigade was selected to accompany the British Army of Occupation into Germany, but Brigades in the IX Corps were not allowed to take their 8-inch batteries to the Rhine. It thus happened that we found ourselves billeted in one of the recently captured French villages with very little to do.

The Army Educational Scheme afforded some diversion, and classes were arranged and well supported until the instructors, one by one, disappeared; sometimes to be demobilised, but more often on being attached to some other unit proceeding to Germany.

At the beginning of December the other batteries in the Brigade took the road for their journey eastward. Colonel Curteis, the Brigade Commander, did not forget to come and say good-bye to the Battery he was leaving behind. He turned up quite unexpectedly one morning and, having lunched with the officers, proceeded to a large hall in the village where the personnel had collected. Speaking with obvious emotion, the Colonel told the men how much he appreciated all the good work they had done; that it was his one regret that he was not to be permitted to take them with him and thus preserve his association with a battery which he had ever felt it an honour to have in his command. He wished officers and men the very best of luck.

There could be no better proof of the esteem in which the Colonel was held by all ranks than the three lusty cheers which the men gave in response to his remarks. Always inquisitive as to their needs and alive to their hardships, Colonel Curteis had deservedly obtained the absolute confidence of the men. The officers, too, had always recognised in their Colonel one who, in the knowledge of his work, was second to no other Brigade Commander in France.

We remained at Wassigny until December 11th, when we moved to a village named Fontaine-au-Pire, which was about half-way between Cambrai and Le Cateau. We managed to have a fairly cheerful time and the Christmas Day festivities were a great success. A real live pig had been purchased at the beginning of December and had since lived with the Battery as one of the family. He was not allotted a regimental number, but was allowed every other privilege, and by the amazing way in which he put on flesh it was clear that he was rapidly qualifying for promotion to the rank of Quartermaster-Sergeant. Unfortunately for him, Christmas intervened and his career was cut short a day or two before December 25th.

We had plenty of sport. The Battery Soccer team made a name for itself by beating all the other batteries in the Brigade. We also started a Rugger team which came on in form so rapidly that it beat a fifteen chosen from the rest of the Brigade. Later on, a tug-of-war team was trained which won the Brigade competition and we were given six out of the eight places in a team which was chosen to represent the Corps H.A.

The officers had guns sent out from England and arranged some jolly shooting parties. They did not succeed in hitting much and would probably have been more successful if they had stuck to the howitzers!

Early in March we supplied a large draft to fill up vacancies in the 25th and 70th Siege Batteries which were going into Germany. Lieutenants Curtis and Webster went to 25 S.B. and Lieutenant Wood to 70 S.B. This left the Major and Lieutenant Jones as the only officers

A Howitzer of the Battery, on View at the Crystal Palace, 1920-21.

in the Battery, as Lieutenant Hobbs had gone up to the Rhine before Christmas, attached to Second Army Headquarters for special legal duties. Lieutenants Gill and Noakes had been posted to other batteries, but were still in the same village with us. Captain Hickson had unfortunately become ill while we were at Wassigny and had been sent home to England.

Our numbers were diminishing daily, and on June 26th the cadre of the Battery, which was about thirty strong, left for England under Lieutenant Jones. The Major thus found himself left with Corporal Dixon and twelve gunners who formed what was called an equipment guard. At last their turn came, and on August 3rd the stores were loaded on the railway at Caudry. Dunkirk was reached on August 6th, and the stores finally loaded on barges for transport to England. Our faithful guns thus went home to a well-earned rest. One of them (No. 765) has since made its appearance at the War Exhibition at the Crystal Palace (1920-21), and can be seen blushing under the admiring gaze of visitors to the exhibition. It is the only 8-inch howitzer there, and its record proves it to be eminently worthy of the distinction thus conferred upon it.

So ends the history of the Battery. The recollection of those days spent in serving the guns will not easily be effaced from the memory of any of us, and the authors plead the pride which its members felt in the achievements of the Battery as an excuse for venturing to place on record the part it played in the War for Freedom and Justice.

APPENDIX A

RECORD OF GUN AT CRYSTAL PALACE.

8-IN. MARK VII HOWITZER.

Calibre	8 inches.
Muzzle velocity	1,500 feet per sec.
Weight of gun and carriage ..	8½ tons.
Weight of projectile	200 lbs.
Maximum range	12,300 yards (7 miles).

WAR SERVICES OF THE EXHIBIT.

(Registered Number 765.)

FOUGHT BY THE 135TH SIEGE BATTERY, ROYAL GARRISON ARTILLERY.

1918 11th January ..	Fired proof rounds at Redesdale. Proceeded to France. Joined Thirteenth Corps.
11th March ..	In position on southern part of Vimy Ridge, N.E. of Arras. Whilst being placed in position the gun was heavily shelled and two officers became casualties.
12th Marth to 24th March.	Constantly in action bombarding German Batteries during the period of artillery activity preceding the German great offensive on this front.
24th March ..	Took part in very interesting shoot on German 5·9 in. Howitzer Battery which had advanced to an exposed position under Vimy Ridge and could be plainly seen from the observation post. At least one of the hostile guns was destroyed and three large explosions of their ammunition were caused.
28th March ..	Enemy great attack on Arras front. North of the River Scarpe. Intense bombardment of the Battery position all day. The pit and cartridge recesses of this howitzer were set on fire, but extinguished by the detachment. Battery withdrawn to Ecurie Station. During the period 12th to 30th March this howitzer fired 737 rounds.
31st March ..	Advanced again to position just north of Ecurie village.

14th April.. ..	To workshops for repairs to cradle.
24th May	Came into action about 1,000 yds. north of Roclincourt. The position became untenable owing to enemy fire.
28th May	Moved in to village of Roclincourt. The howitzer was well concealed among trees and ruins, and though continually shooting was never discovered.
21st July	Moved to position in valley east of Souchez.
6th August ..	In position in valley S.E. of Gentelles Wood, east of Amiens, in support of the Canadian Corps, who had the French on their right.
8th August ..	Took part in bombardment (firing 120 rounds) and in the advance halting "in readiness" at Hamon Wood (4 miles).
13th August ..	In action just north of Folies. Removed to workshops for damaged piston-rod.
17th September ..	In action in valley between Attilly and St. Quentin Wood. (This was a very "rough spot" at that time.)
18th September ..	Supported the unsuccessful attack on the outworks of the Hindenburg Line round Fresnoy-le-Petit.
21st and 22nd September ..	During a heavy concentration of enemy fire on the Valley (about 3,000 rounds) this howitzer remained unharmed, though its neighbour was knocked out.
24th September ..	Attack of the 18th repeated. Fired 74 rounds on hostile batteries.
25th September ..	Moved to N.W. corner St. Quentin Wood.
29th September ..	Supported great attack on Hindenburg Line through Bellenglise. During period from 27th to 29th September this howitzer fired 569 rounds, chiefly on hostile batteries.
3rd & 4th October	Advanced to position just north of Magny-la-Fosse (9½ miles).
8th October ..	Took part in attack on enemy positions west of Bohain, bombarding enemy batteries. At night advanced to Ramicourt (3½ miles).
12th October ..	In position north of liberated town of Bohain.
17th October ..	Supported the attack which drove the enemy from his position between Bohain and Andigny-les-Fermes, firing 74 rounds on hostile batteries.

31st October ..	In action in position east of Ribeauville.
4th November to 11th November.	Took part in last battle of the war, when enemy in this sector were driven from their positions along the Oise Canal and kept moving until the Armistice.
	During the whole above period the howitzer fired 5,276 rounds. After the Armistice the howitzer moved to Fontaine-au-Pire, near Cambrai, till 4th August, 1919.
1919 8th August ..	Loaded on a barge at Dunkirk and despatched to England.

LIST OF OFFICERS WHO SERVED WITH THE 135TH SIEGE BATTERY,

ROYAL GARRISON ARTILLERY, DURING THIS PERIOD.

Captain (Acting Major) C. P. HEATH, D.S.O., R.G.A.
Captain C. E. LUCAS PHILLIPS, M.C., R.G.A.
Captain H. HICKSON, R.G.A.
Lieut. K. F. ALLEN, R.G.A.
Lieut. J. W. CURTIS, R.G.A.
Lieut. W. D. HOOPER, R.G.A.
Lieut. F. A. STEVENS, R.G.A.
Lieut. R. PHAUP, R.G.A.
Lieut. W. R. JONES, R.G.A.
Lieut. T. R. WOOD, R.G.A.
Lieut. E. HILL, R.G.A.
Lieut. E. J. NOAKES, R.G.A.
Lieut. C. R. H. HOBBS, R.G.A.
Lieut. O. L. GILL, R.G.A.
Lieut. W. H. MEARS, R.G.A.
Lieut. R. A. HOWELL, R.A.S.C.
Lieut. J. BEAVAN, R.A.S.C.

APPENDIX B

ROLL OF HONOUR.

R.G.A. PERSONNEL.

Regtl. No.	Rank.	Name.	Casualty.	Where Buried.
74491	Gnr.	Kershaw H.	At Longueval, 3/10/16	Military Cemetery, near Montauban (Somme).
77475	,,	Metcalf, E.	At Longueval, 8/10/16	
77454	,,	Senior, B.	From wounds received at Longueval, 8/10/16	
30936	Cpl.	Tapping, W.	Wounded at O.P. near Rancourt, 13/2/17, Died 6/3/17.	From Hospital.
23243	B.Q.M.S.	Hawkins, J.	At Arras, 4/4/17	Military Cemetery, Arras.
64690	Gnr.	Lewis R.	Died of wounds received at Feuchy Chapel, 20/4/17	
78026	,,	Burdock, E.		
	2nd Lt.	Goodwin, H. J.	At Feuchy Chapel, 24/4/17	Military Cemetery, Arras :
67203	Gnr.	Hill, J. E.		Row C, Plot 5, No. 1.
79052	,,	Lamb, W. A.		Row C, Plot 5, No. 2.
				Row C, Plot 5, No. 3.
73049	,,	Robson, W.	Died of wounds received at Feuchy Chapel, 30/4/17	Military Cemetery, Arras.
128238	S./Gnr.	Rawlinson, H.	Near Nieuport, 2/8/17	Coxyde Cemetery.
96495	Gnr.	Davies, A.	Near Nieuport, 7/9/17	Coxyde Cemetery.
73052	,,	Coates, T.	Died of wounds received near Nieuport, 28/10/17	From Hospital.
104595	,,	Kenworthy, G.	Near Nieuport, 10/11/17	Coxyde Cemetery : Grave 1, Plot 4, Row L.

Regtl. No.	Rank.	Name.	Casualty.	Where Buried.
94972	Gnr.	Burgess, W.	Near Nieuport, 14/11/17	Coxyde Cemetery.
66625	"	Mackay, B. J.	Wounded near Bailleul (Vimy Ridge), 27/2/18. Died 28/2/18.	Maroeuil Cemetery: Plot 4, Row H, No. 8.
69475	Bdr.	Gricewood, C.	Wounded near Bailleul (Vimy Ridge), 27/2/18. Died 29/2/18.	Maroeuil Cemetery: Plot 4, Row H, No. 7.
376205	Gnr.	Lynch, W.	Died of wounds received at Bailleul, 12/3/18.	From Hospital.
85213	"	Williams, T.	Near Roclincourt, 14/3/18	Roclincourt Cemetery: Plot 6, Row A, No. 9.
107393	"	Herbert, H. W.	Wounded at "X2" Position, 26/3/18. Died 18/4/18.	From Hospital.
77460	Cpl.	Jackson, J. E.	Wounded at "X2" Position, 28/3/18. Died 28/3/18.	Roclincourt Cemetery: Plot 4, Row B, No. 12.
172843	Gnr.	Townsend, M.	Wounded at "X2" Position, 28/3/18. Died 4/4/18.	
21810	"	Douglas, T.	Died of wounds received at Plank Road (near Roclincourt), 18/5/18.	
177259	"	Taylor, H. B.	Wounded at Plank Road, 18/5/18. Died 20/5/18.	
59182	"	Dickerson, V.	Near Attilly, 18/9/18	Near Villeveque.
105552	"	Woolley, W.	At Magny-la-Fosse, 6/10/18	Bellenglise Cemetery.
195296	"	Wade, T.	Died of wounds received at Bohain, 18/10/18.	
213303	"	Brace, F.	At Ribeauville, 31/10/18.	Near Ribeauville.

APPENDIX C

BATTLE CASUALTIES (WOUNDED). OFFICERS. R.G.A.

Rank.	Name.	Casualty.	Date.
2nd Lieut.	Minns, W.	Hospital, wounded (shell gas)	13/3/18
2nd Lieut.	Wood, S. R.	Hospital, wounded (shell gas)	13/3/18
2nd Lieut.	Hill, E.	Hospital, wounded	13/3/18
2nd Lieut.	Jones, W. R.	Hospital, wounded (shell gas)	18/3/18
2nd Lieut.	Wood, T. R.	Hospital, wounded	18/9/18
2nd Lieut.	Hobbs, C. R. H.	Remained at Duty	19/9/18

BATTLE CASUALTIES (WOUNDED). OTHER RANKS. R.G.A.

Regtl. No.	Rank.	Name.	Casualty.	Date.
79088	A./Bdr.	Carr, R.	Admitted Hospital, wounded	5/10/16
77350	Gnr.	Brooks, H.	Wounded. To Hospital	8/10/16
62430	,,	Wood, H.	Admitted Hospital, wounded	9/10/16
77444	,,	Bass, G.	Wounded. To Hospital	17/11/16
79126	A./Bdr.	Baxter, N.	Wounded. To Hospital	24/11/16
64345	Gnr.	Taylor, O.	Admitted Hospital, wounded	9/ 2/17
6644	B.S.M.	Banfield, F.	Admitted Hospital, wounded	4/ 4/17
103837	Gnr.	Falkingham, C.	Admitted Hospital, wounded	6/ 4/17
38002	Sgt.	Napper, F.	Admitted Hospital, wounded	8/ 4/17
79685	Gnr.	West, A.	Admitted Hospital, wounded	14/ 4/17

Regtl. No.	Rank.	Name.	Casualty.	Date.
55835	Gnr.	Keely, H.	Admitted Hospital, wounded	15/ 4/17
79083	,,	Tully, P.	Admitted Hospital, wounded	17/ 4/17
64690	,,	Lewis, R.	Admitted Hospital, wounded	19/ 4/17
78974	,,	Mannings, E.	Admitted Hospital, wounded	21/ 4/17
33484	,,	Maddock, H.	Admitted Hospital, wounded	22/ 4/17
77458	,,	Dodd, S.	Admitted Hospital, wounded	22/ 4/17
52069	,,	Devine, C.	Admitted Hospital, wounded	22/ 4/17
27234	,,	Neill, J. G.	Admitted Hospital, wounded	22/ 4/17
83861	,,	Smith, B.	Admitted Hospital, wounded	23/ 4/17
77318	,,	Johnson, G.	Admitted Hospital, wounded	23/ 4/17
74510	,,	Wesmorland, H.	Admitted Hospital, wounded	23/ 4/17
73052	,,	Coates, T.	Admitted Hospital, wounded	29/ 4/17
73049	,,	Robson, W.	Admitted Hospital, wounded	30/ 4/17
77421	,,	Manners, F.	Admitted Hospital, wounded	2/ 5/17
79093	,,	Child, J.	Admitted Hospital, wounded	5/ 5/17
98556	,,	Powlesland	Admitted Hospital, wounded	9/ 5/17
132924	Cpl.	Clemence, H.	Admitted Hospital, wounded	16/ 5/17
67042	A./Bdr.	Thompson, W.	Admitted Hospital, wounded	23/ 5/17
65773	Sgt.	Hansell, H.	Admitted Hospital, wounded	20/ 6/17
104094	Gnr.	Crewe, H.	Admitted Hospital, wounded	13/ 7/17
73747	,,	Hughes, H.	Admitted Hospital, wounded	13/ 7/17
77321	,,	Mitcheson, J.	Admitted Hospital, wounded	13/ 7/17
92572	,,	Wickenden, C.	Wounded slightly, remained at duty	17/ 7/17
80937	,,	Greenfield, J.	Wounded slightly, remained at duty	20/ 7/17
63531	,,	Atkinson, J.	Admitted Hospital, wounded (gas)	30/ 7/17
114732	,,	Holloway, W.	Admitted Hospital, wounded (gas)	30/ 7/17
138271	,,	Collinson, G.	Wounded slightly, remained at duty	8/ 8/17

110197	Gnr.	Varcoe, A.	Admitted Hospital, wounded	21/ 8/17
275338	A./Bdr.	Butler, G.	Admitted Hospital, wounded	21/ 8/17
148875	Gnr.	Carrington, C.	Admitted Hospital, wounded	26/ 8/17
121603	A./Bdr.	Inglis, D.	Admitted Hospital, wounded	26/ 8/17
77409	Gnr.	Smith, G.	Admitted Hospital, wounded	3/ 9/17
6031	B.Q.M.S.	Chapell, H.	Admitted Hospital, wounded	3/ 9/17
79093	Gnr.	Child, J.	Admitted Hospital, wounded	3/ 9/17
72954	,,	Lewis, S.	Admitted Hospital, wounded	8/ 9/17
79144	,,	Lancaster, G.	Admitted Hospital, wounded	8/ 9/17
66947	,,	Collins, E.	Admitted Hospital, wounded	8/ 9/17
319205	,,	Trench, T.	Admitted Hospital, wounded	19/ 9/17
143300	,,	Lawton, W.	Admitted Hospital, wounded	19/ 9/17
79348	,,	Fielder, R.	Wounded, remained at duty	27/ 9/17
77421	,,	Manners, F.	Admitted Hospital, wounded	2/10/17
30542	A./Cpl.	Harding, J.	Wounded, remained at duty	12/10/17
69233	Bdr.	Purvis, W.	Admitted Hospital, wounded	13/10/17
77461	Cpl.	Randall, W.	Admitted Hospital, wounded	13/10/17
77447	Gnr.	Pashley, T.	Admitted Hospital, wounded	28/10/17
79058	,,	Price, F.	Admitted Hospital, wounded	10/11/17
80853	,,	Chapman, R.	Admitted Hospital, wounded	23/11/17
120827	,,	Payne, A.	Admitted Hospital, wounded	26/12/17
147743	,,	Hughes, A.	Admitted Hospital, wounded	10/ 1/18
95049	,,	Pacey, L.	Admitted Hospital, wounded	27/ 2/18
171003	,,	Coy, P.	Hospital, shell gas	5/ 3/18
159242	,,	Culm, F.	Hospital, shell gas	5/ 3/18
77346	Cpl.	Mauchlin, G.	Hospital, shell gas	5/ 3/18
8550	,,	Reynolds, A.	Hospital, shell gas	5/ 3/18
334412	Gnr.	Stone, A.	Hospital, shell gas	5/ 3/18
169894	,,	Sharp, P.	Hospital, shell gas	5/ 3/18
3653	,,	Daly, P.	Hospital, shell gas	5/ 3/18
171103	,,	Higgins, R.	Hospital, shell gas	6/ 3/18

Regtl. No.	Rank.	Name.	Casualty.	Date.
39959	Bdr.	Waughman, H.	Hospital, shell gas	6/ 3/18
77409	,,	Smith, G.	Hospital, shell gas	6/ 3/18
77443	Gnr.	Martin, J.	Hospital, shell gas	6/ 3/18
77476	,,	Robinson, G.	Hospital, shell gas	6/ 3/18
141208	,,	Llewellyn, G.	Hospital, shell gas	6/ 3/18
161646	,,	Cliff, G.	Hospital, shell gas	6/ 3/18
77333	,,	Weight, L.	Hospital, shell gas	6/ 3/18
82338	,,	Hodgkinson, R.	Hospital, shell gas	7/ 3/18
72982	,,	Townsend, A.	Hospital, shell gas	7/ 3/18
170421	,,	McKeon, J.	Hospital, shell gas	7/ 3/18
141448	,,	Juggins, E.	Hospital, shell gas	7/ 3/18
77466	,,	Worrall, A.	Hospital, shell gas	10/ 3/18
49530	,,	Brown, M.	Hospital, shell gas	10/ 3/18
296689	F./Gnr.	Rumble, A.	Hospital, shell gas	10/ 3/18
109873	Gnr.	Cox, A.	Admitted Hospital, wounded	10/ 3/18
77443	,,	Martin, J.	Admitted Hospital, wounded and gassed	11/ 3/18
340948	,,	Derrick, A.	Admitted Hospital, wounded and gassed	12/ 3/18
74534	,,	Deeming, A.	Admitted Hospital, N.Y.D. gas	12/ 3/18
147265	,,	Timms, W. H.	Admitted Hospital, N.Y.D. gas	12/ 3/18
144931	,,	Kerby, F.	Admitted Hospital, N.Y.D. gas	12/ 3/18
79125	,,	Bonner, E.	Admitted Hospital, N.Y.D. gas	12/ 3/18
53871	,,	Foster, E.	Admitted Hospital, wounded	12/ 3/18
94384	,,	Goodridge, H.	Admitted Hospital, wounded	12/ 3/18
123581	,,	Hulme, F.	Admitted Hospital, wounded	12/ 3/18
77031	,,	Entwistle, E.	Admitted Hospital, wounded	12/ 3/18
194318	,,	Hollingsworth, H.	Admitted Hospital, wounded	12/ 3/18
72933	,,	Morland, A.	Admitted Hospital, wounded	12/ 3/18

120438	Gnr.	Giles, L.	Admitted Hospital, wounded	12/ 3/18
77465	Cpl.	Jackson, W.	Admitted Hospital, wounded	12/ 3/18
277746	,,	Coull, C.	Admitted Hospital, wounded and gassed ..	13/ 3/18
277429	Bdr.	Waghorn, W.	Admitted Hospital, wounded and gassed ..	13/ 3/18
119091	Gnr.	Selfe, F.	Admitted Hospital, wounded and gassed ..	13/ 3/18
190056	,,	Hawkins, F.	Admitted Hospital, wounded and gassed ..	13/ 3/18
19074	,,	Weekly, M.	Admitted Hospital, wounded and gassed ..	13/ 3/18
107590	,,	Ilott, S.	Admitted Hospital, wounded and gassed ..	13/ 3/18
138271	,,	Collinson, G.	Gas, 13/3/18. To Hospital	14/ 3/18
65773	Sgt.	Hansell, H.	Admitted Hospital, wounded and gassed ..	14/ 3/18
57665	A./Sgt.	Slinger, H.	Admitted Hospital, wounded and gassed ..	14/ 3/18
104137	Bdr.	Medley, H.	Admitted Hospital, wounded and gassed ..	14/ 3/18
61351	Gnr.	Cross, W.	Admitted Hospital, wounded and gassed ..	14/ 3/18
166633	,,	Winter, W.	Admitted Hospital, wounded	17/ 3/18
54727	Sgt.	Burns, E.	Admitted Hospital, wounded	18/ 3/18
66947	Gnr.	Collins, E.	Admitted Hospital, wounded	18/ 3/18
88180	,,	Knott, W.	Admitted Hospital, wounded	18/ 3/18
143711	,,	Bull, W.	Admitted Hospital, wounded	18/ 3/18
15716	,,	Land, R.	Admitted Hospital, wounded, shell gas ..	20/ 3/18
118990	,,	Langer, W.	Admitted Hospital, wounded, shell gas ..	20/ 3/18
38750	,,	Rodgers, A.	Admitted Hospital, wounded, shell gas ..	20/ 3/18
39537	,,	Whelan, T.	Admitted Hospital, wounded, ...	21/ 3/18
316140	Bdr.	Jarvis, A.	Admitted Hospital, wounded, shell gas ..	21/ 3/18
115683	Gnr.	Stoner, W.	Admitted Hospital, wounded, shell gas ..	21/ 3/18
177459	,,	Wallis, F.	Admitted Hospital, wounded, shell gas ..	21/ 3/18
139992	,,	Byrne, T.	Admitted Hospital, wounded, shell gas ..	21/ 3/18
96831	,,	Mills, G.	Admitted Hospital, wounded, shell gas ..	21/ 3/18
80725	,,	Alvey, W.	Admitted Hospital, wounded, shell gas ..	21/ 3/18
177036	,,	Walker, P.	Admitted Hospital, wounded, shell gas ..	21/ 3/18
123885	,,	Taylor, W. H.	Admitted Hospital, wounded, shell gas ..	21/ 3/18
24668	,,	O'Brien, P.	Admitted Hospital, wounded, shell gas ..	22/ 3/18

Regtl. No.	Rank.	Name.	Casualty.	Date.
173612	Sgt.	Irvine, W.	Admitted Hospital, wounded, shell gas	22/ 3/18
107032	Gnr.	Gallop, J.	Admitted Hospital, wounded, shell gas	22/ 3/18
166304	,,	Skinner, F.	Admitted Hospital, wounded, shell gas	22/ 3/18
105560	,,	Jones, L.	Admitted Hospital, wounded, shell gas	22/ 3/18
77142	Sgt.	Darby, F.	Admitted Hospital, wounded, shell gas	25/ 3/18
61078	Gnr.	Gellatly, R.	Admitted Hospital, wounded, shell gas	25/ 3/18
30542	Cpl.	Harding, J.	Admitted Hospital, wounded, shell gas	25/ 3/18
101410	Gnr.	Dove, W.	Admitted Hospital, wounded	28/ 3/18
39093	,,	Child, J.	Admitted Hospital, wounded	28/ 3/18
181504	,,	Clough, W.	Admitted Hospital, wounded	28/ 3/18
106936	,,	Iliffe, N.	Admitted Hospital, wounded	28/ 3/18
120192	,,	Hill, T.	Admitted Hospital, wounded	28/ 3/18
172436	,,	Styles, E.	Admitted Hospital, wounded	28/ 3/18
70060	,,	Morton, W.	Admitted Hospital, wounded	28/ 3/18
77326	,,	Chapman, W.	Admitted Hospital, wounded, shell gas	12/ 4/18
156570	A./Bdr.	Collyer, E.	Admitted Hospital, wounded, shell gas	12/ 4/18
186039	Gnr.	Davenport, G.	Admitted Hospital, wounded	17/ 5/18
141208	,,	Llewellyn, G.	Admitted Hospital, wounded	17/ 5/18
182800	,,	Gordon, J.	Admitted Hospital, wounded	17/ 5/18
127875	,,	Taylor, M.	Admitted Hospital, wounded	17/ 5/18
113720	,,	Rimmer, J.	Admitted Hospital, wounded	17/ 5/18
96537	,,	Cartwright, G.	Wounded, remained at duty	17/ 5/18
75618	Cpl.	Burnett, H.	Wounded, remained at duty	17/ 5/18
55490	Sgt.	Baldwin, A.	Wounded, remained at duty	18/ 5/18
185877	Gnr.	Hadwin, J.	Admitted Hospital, wounded	18/ 5/18
86697	,,	Wiltshire, H.	Admitted Hospital, wounded	18/ 5/18
79144	A./Bdr.	Lancaster, G.	Admitted Hospital, wounded	15/ 9/18

30542	Cpl.	Harding, J.	Admitted Hospital, wounded	16/ 9/18
150680	Gnr.	Brodie, T.	Admitted Hospital, wounded	18/ 9/18
165664	,,	Kingdon, J.	Admitted Hospital, wounded	18/ 9/18
95001	,,	Hassell, E.	Admitted Hospital, wounded	18/ 9/18
69205	,,	Ibbotson, H.	Admitted Hospital, wounded	18/ 9/18
352872	Sgt.	Anderson, H.	Admitted Hospital, wounded	22/ 9/18
77446	Gnr.	Hepworth, A.	Admitted Hospital, wounded	22/ 9/18
139536	,,	Spooner, W.	Admitted Hospital, wounded	22/ 9/18
374459	F./Gnr.	Hopkins, F.	Admitted Hospital, wounded	22/ 9/18
171577	Gnr.	Fenton, A.	Admitted Hospital, wounded	22/ 9/18
176209	,,	Lawson, W.	Admitted Hospital, gas	22/ 9/18
296894	,,	Kinder, R.	Admitted Hospital, gas	22/ 9/18
134757	,,	Overton, L.	Admitted Hospital, gas	22/ 9/18
166726	,,	Swindley, J.	Admitted Hospital, gas	22/ 9/18
275448	A./Bdr.	Sexton, J.	Admitted Hospital, gas	22/ 9/18
103836	Cpl.	Hinchliffe, G.	Admitted Hospital, wounded	22/ 9/18
77421	Gnr.	Manners, F.	Wounded, remained at duty	23/ 9/18
67430	,,	Gray, J.	Admitted Hospital, gas	24/ 9/18
113267	,,	Doughty, H.	Admitted Hospital, wounded	6/10/18
101608	,,	Smith, J.	Admitted Hospital, wounded	6/10/18
109778	,,	Pearson, W.	Admitted Hospital, wounded	6/10/18
506733	,,	Tucker, S.	Admitted Hospital, gas	7/10/18
76586	Sgt.	Marsh	Admitted Hospital, wounded	31/10/18
110943	Gnr.	Wright, F.	Admitted Hospital, wounded	31/10/18

R.A.O.C. ATTACHED.

	S./Sgt.	Band	Wounded	–/ 6/17

R.F.C. ATTACHED.

9707	1st A.M.	Broome, W.	Wounded, shell gas	14/ 3/18

APPENDIX D

MONTHLY SUMMARY OF CASUALTIES.

Year	Month	Killed	Wounded	Gassed	Total	Remarks
1916	Aug.	—	—	—	0	Somme.
	Sept.	—	—	—	0	
	Oct.	3	3	—	6	
	Nov.	—	2	—	2	
	Dec.	—	—	—	0	Combles.
1917	Jan.	—	—	—	0	
	Feb.	1	1	—	2	
	March	—	—	—	0	
	April	7	15	—	22	Arras Attack.
	May	—	5	—	5	
	June	—	2	—	2	Tilloy.
	July	—	5	2	7	Dunes, near Nieuport.
	Aug.	1	5	—	6	
	Sept.	1	9	—	10	
	Oct.	2	5	—	7	
	Nov.	1	2	—	3	
	Dec.	—	1	—	1	
1918	Jan.	—	1	—	1	"X2" and "M."
	Feb.	2	2	—	4	
	March	5	22	59	86	"X2" and "S."
	April	—	—	2	2	Ecurie, Plank Road, Roclincourt and Souchez.
	May	2	10	—	12	
	June	—	—	—	0	
	July	—	—	—	0	
	Aug.	—	—	—	0	Advance from Amiens.
	Sept.	1	13	6	20	
	Oct.	3	5	1	9	
Totals ..		29	108	70	207	

APPENDIX E

SUMMARY OF AMMUNITION EXPENDED, 1916.

Day of Month.	Aug.	Sept.	Oct.	Nov.	Dec.
1			—	18	
2			9	31	
3			3	24	
4			7	61	
5			51	235	
6			300	41	
7			550	44	
8			100	59	
9			70	20	
10			100	205	Battery Moving.
11			428	—	
12			478	100	
13			0	49	
14			2	162	
15	No Records available.		46	50	
16			180	22	
17			102	4	
18			220	—	
19			144	—	
20			10	112	
21			237	50	—
22			506	50	15
23			539		3
24			338		8
25			125		—
26			137		24
27			47		25
28			195		1
29			275		—
30			205		35
31		—	70	—	12
		Totals ..	5,474	1,337	123

SUMMARY OF AMMUNITION EXPENDED, 1917.

Day of Month.	January.	February.	March.	April.	May.	June.	July.	August.	September.	October.	November.	December.
1	0	4	57	40	153	94	18	No Record.	51	208	No. Record.	—
2	0	0	100	10	226	100	0		237	74		—
3	15	0	50	14	656	206	0		—	20		
4	0	16	256	184	176	120	0		288	156		Move
5	11	100	30	232	90	100	30		0	227		
6	0	0	—	136	343	37	Move to Nieuport.		3	No. Record.		
7	0	0	6	314	130	93			No. Record.			
8	0	0	—	194	35	29						
9	0	31	—	563	0	80						
10	0	200	—	309	No Record.	88						
11	0	0	—	141		24						
12	14	320	—	4		3						Week 75
13	3	50	40	13		31						
14	0	4	50	166		541						
15	0	214	—	122		69						
16	0	7	100	87		276						
17	0	310	Move to Arras.	116		234	No Record.	219				
18	0	25		30		261		184				
19	13	0		144		100		107				Week 36
20	0	0		209		80		145				
21	34	0		247		4		100				
22	0	0		135		32		100				
23	13	0		577		76		100	0			
24	50	75		240		5		0	6			
25	16	90	9	159		0		47	95			
26	34	120	0	0		36		100	31		For Week 160	Week 96
27	37	150	0	448		75		7	160			
28	116	54	0	520		0		0	125			
29	31	—	0	40		29		20	62			
30	0	—	20	210		0		17	161			
31	12	—	0	—	24	—		157	—		—	
Totals	399	1,770	718	5,604	—	2,823	—	—	—	—	—	207

SUMMARY OF AMMUNITION EXPENDED, 1918.

Day of Month.	January.	February.	March.	April.	May.	June.	July.	August.	September.	October.	November
	Week										
1		135	10	137	62	45	No Record.	Move to Gentelles Wood.	No Record.	No Firing.	0
2		70	0	150	20	157					6
3		106	50	147	40	15					42
4	165	50	19	305	20	6				—	762
5		263	178	176	91	0			Rest at Amiens. and Moves.	25	0
6		325	0	33	21	2				192	0
7		0	40	200	24	0				155	0
8		38	212	54	2	0		700		300	0
9		86	43	178	13	No Record.		No Firing.		25	0
10	147	32	109	209	5					200	0
11		0	223	160	28					0	Armistice.
12		13	131	104	1					0	
13		2	464	379	16					11	
14	Battery at rest.	0	10	27	0					150	
15		0	53	92	116					80	
16		164	150	167	58			No Record.		25	
17		227	321	130	4					290	
18		197	154	93	30				404	No Firing.	
19		150	0	55	29				No Record.		
20		76	0	75	9						
21		19	208	248	181						
22		0	58	193	160						
23		0	394	63	44				410		
24		85	239	20	17				459		
25		33	102	20	104				104		
26		78	315	0	9				0		
27		108	47	20	180			No Firing.	625		
28		178	800	11	174				625		
29			90	30	100				857		
30	—		343	26	178				0		
31	20		—		14			—			
Total	332	2,435	4,763	3,502	1,750	—	—	—	—	1,453	810

Note.—The figures up to June give the Totals fired by the two separate Halves of the Battery.

APPENDIX F

RECORD OF THE 83RD BRIGADE, R.G.A. AUGUST 8TH—NOVEMBER 11TH, 1918.

Employment of Brigade.	Date.	Rounds.	Remarks.	Battle Casualties. Killed. O.	Killed. O.R.	Wounded. O.	Wounded. O.R.
Bombardment Domart, Canadian Corps.	Aug. 8th, 1918	5,112	Fourth Army attack ..	—	1	—	1
Moving battle, 60-pdr. and 6-in. in support of 3rd Canadian Division, and 32nd Division.	" 9th, "	713 .. .. 200 (German)*	Attack by 3rd Canadian Division. Beaufort and Folies captured.	—	—	—	
	" 10th, "	1,062					
	" 11th, "	4,299	Attack on Parvillers ..	—	—	—	4
	" 12th, "	978		—	—	—	1
	" 13th, "	413		—	—	—	1
	" 14th, "	815 .. .. 100 (German)*		—	—	—	1
	" 15th, "	1,036 .. .. 100 (German)*		—	—	—	2
Heavy Batteries in position. Brigade under Command of Canadian Corps.	" 16th, "	2,719 .. .. 890 (German)*	Parvillers occupied ..	—	2	—	7
	" 17th, " "	2,860 .. .. 1,080 (German)*		—	—	—	1
	" 18th, "	2,310 .. .. 1,160 (German)*		—	—	—	1
	" 19th, "	2,046		—	—	—	3
	" 20th, "	2,955					
	" 21st, "	3,368					

* German 15 cm. Hows. and 10 cm. Guns collected and manned by Brigade.

	,, 22nd, ,,	879		—	—	—	1
Heavy Batteries in position. Brigade under Command of XXXI French Corps.	,, 23rd, ,,	1,012		—	—	—	—
	,, 24th, ,,	898		—	—	—	—
	,, 25th, ,,	394		—	—	—	—
	,, 26th, ,,	1,639	Fresnoy captured ..	—	—	—	—
Moving Battle. Brigade in support of French 47th and 126th Divisions.	,, 27th, ,,	3,034	Roye occupied	—	—	—	—
	,, 28th, ,,	807	Nesle captured	—	—	—	—
	,, 29th, ,,	1,420		—	—	—	—
	,, 30th, ,,	1,669		—	—	—	5
	,, 31st, ,,	1,510		—	1	9	37
Heavy Batteries in position. Brigade under Command of XXXI French Corps.	Sept. 1st, ,,	742	Canal S.E. of Nesle crossed in places. ..	—	1	—	2
	,, 2nd, ,,	762		—	—	—	—
	,, 3rd, ,,	1,280		—	4	—	3
	,, 4th, ,,	2,728		—	3	—	—
	,, 5th, ,,	400	Canal crossed and advance resumed. Ham captured.	1	7	—	—
	Brigade out of	Line 6th to 15th.					
	,, 16th, ,,	—		—	4	—	7
	,, 18th, ,,	2,691	Attack on whole Corps Front. Fresnoy and Gricourt taken.	—	1	1	16
	,, 19th, ,,	2,822		2	—	1	—
Heavy Batteries in position. Brigade under Command of IX Corps. W. and N.W. of St. Quentin Wood.	,, 20th, ,,	2,699		—	1	—	10
	,, 21st, ,,	2,932		—	—	—	1
	,, 22nd, ,,	2,873		—	4	1	35
	,, 23rd, ,,	2,870		—	—	—	4
	,, 24th, ,,	3,112	Attack on Corps front. Some progress.	—	1	—	5

Employment of Brigade.	Date.	Rounds.	Remarks.	Battle Casualties.			
				Killed.		Wounded.	
				O.	O.R.	O.	O.R.
Heavy Batteries in position. Brigade under Command of IX Co-ps. W. and N.W. of St. Quentin Wood.	Sept. 25th, 1918	2,930		—	—	—	3
	„ 26th, „	804		—	—	—	—
	„ 27th, „	4,006	Bombardment Hindenburg Line.	—	—	—	—
	„ 28th, „	4,006					
	„ 29th, „	10,866	Hindenburg Line taken. Bellinglese, etc., captured.	—	—	—	—
Moving Battle. Brigade in support of 46th and 6th Divisions.	„ 30th, „	2,713	Thorigny captured ..	—	—	—	3
	Oct. 1st, „	1,470		—	—	1	7
	„ 2nd, „	2,050		—	1	—	—
Heavy Batteries in position. Brigade under Command of IX Corps and affiliated to 46th sion.	„ 3rd, „	1,850	Attack on Fonsomme-Beaurevoir Line. Line broken N. of Sequehart by 46th Division.	—	—	—	4
	„ 4th, „	3,037	Sequehart taken and retaken several times.				
	„ 5th, „	2,140		—	—	—	4
	„ 6th, „	2,270		—	1	—	3
	„ 7th, „	1,800		—	—	—	1
	„ 8th, „	3,020	Montbrehain, Brancourt, etc., captured.	—	3	—	7
Moving Battle. Brigade in support of 6th Division.	„ 9th. „	2,500	Line advanced to E. of Bohain.	—	1	—	—
	„ 10th, „	1,018		—	—	—	—
	„ 11th, „	700	Attack by 6th Division.	—	—	—	—
	„ 12th, „	1,236	Attack by 18th Infantry Brigade.	—	4	—	6
	„ 13th, „	650		—	1	—	—

Heavy Batteries in position. Brigade under Command of IX Corps.	„ 14th, „	1,600	Bombardment of Vaux-Andigny Line.	—	—	—	—
	„ 15th, „	1,608					
	„ 16th, „	1,360					
	„ 17th, „	3,103	Attack by Fourth Army. 1st Division reach Wassigny.	—	—	—	4
Moving Battle. Brigade in support of 1st Division.	„ 18th, „	2,053	Attack and capture of Wassigny.	—	1	1	—
	„ 19th, „	850		—	—	—	1
	„ 20th, „	900	Enemy mostly on East side of Canal.	1	—	—	—
	„ 21st, „	972		—	—	—	—
	„ 22nd, „	1,100		—	—	—	1
	„ 23rd, „	2,810	Enemy finally driven across Canal, except round Catillon.	—	1	—	4
	„ 24th, „	1,620		—	—	—	10
	„ 25th, „	1,750		—	—	—	—
Heavy Batteries in position. Brigade under Command of IX Corps.	Nov. 4th, „	6,900	Attack on 90 km. Front. 1st Division crossed Canal and advanced well beyond it.	—	1	—	—
	„ 5th and 6th		Waiting for bridge at Catillon.	—	—	—	—
Moving Battle. Brigade in support of 46th Division.	„ 7th, 1918	70	Prisches, Cartignies and Avesnes captured.	—	—	—	—
	„ 8th, „	900	Enemy running.. ..	—	1	—	—
		150,051		4	45	14	206
			Total Casualties, all ranks				269

70 DAYS' FIGHTING, AVERAGE 2,144 ROUNDS PER DAY.

The Brigade was in touch with the enemy and shooting every day it was in the line, except for two days (November 5th and 6th) of enforced waiting for the completion of the bridge at Catillon.

During the period October 22nd, 1917 to November 11th, 1918, the Brigade lost in action :—

7 Officers killed.
34 ,, wounded.
76 O.R. killed.
600 ,, wounded.

Total Battle Casualties, 717.

For the same period, the Honours and Rewards were :—

1 C.M.G.
1 Brevet.
1 D.S.O.
10 M.C.'s.
1 Bar to M.C.
7 D.C.M.'s.
43 M.M.'s.
2 Bar to M.M.'s.
6 M.S.M.'s.
25 Mentions.
8 Foreign Decorations.
4 Foreign Mentions.

APPENDIX G

NOMINAL ROLL OF OFFICERS OF 135th SIEGE BATTERY, R.G.A.

RANK.	NAME.	RANK.	NAME.
Lieut.	Curtis, J. W.	2nd Lieut.	Minns, W.
Lieut.	Gill, O. L.	Lieut.	Noakes, E. J.
2nd Lieut.	Goodwin, H. J.	Lieut.	Phaup, R.
Capt.	Heath, C. P., D.S.O.	Capt.	Phillips, C. E. L., M.C.
(Actg. Major)		Lieut.	Reid.
Capt.	Hickson, H.	2nd Lieut.	Richardson, E. G.
2nd Lieut.	Hill, E.	Major	Sladen, D. B. C., D.S.O.
Lieut.	Hobbs, C. R. H.	2nd Lieut.	Stevens, F. A.
Lieut.	Hooper, W. D.	Lieut.	Walters, D. J., M.C.
Lieut.	Jones, W. R.	2nd Lieut.	Webster, J. L.
2nd Lieut.	Little.	Lieut.	Wood, S. R.
2nd Lieut.	Mears, W. H.	Lieut.	Wood, T. R.

A.S.C. OFFICERS ATTACHED.

Lieut. Howell, R. A.
Lieut. Beavan.

APPENDIX G

NOMINAL ROLL OF MEN OF 135th SIEGE BATTERY R.G.A.

Name.	Name.	Name.
Adams, A. W.	Boucher, G.	Clements, G.
Adams, F. R.	Boulding, J. N.	Clift, G.
Ainsworth, J. S.	Boxall, E.	Clough, W.
Alcock, W. J.	Boyers, C. E.	Coates, T.
Alder, L. C.	Brace, F.	Coles, H.
Allan, D., M.M.	Branch, A.	Collins, E.
Allbright, J.	Brazier, T.	Collinson, G.
Allen, A. G.	Brewitt, J. C.	Collyer, E. H.
Allen, J.	Bridgewater, J. C.	Connor, C. W.
Allport, W. H.	Briggs, W.	Coope, T.
Almond, E. S.	Brodie, T. D.	Cooper, J.
Alvey, W.	Brooks, H. W.	Coull, C.
Andas, W.	Brown, A. H.	County, A.
Anderson, H. W.	Brown, F. F.	Cox, A. G.
Arch, E.	Brown, M. R.	Coy, P.
Armstrong, G.	Brown, R. W.	Crawley, A. G.
Ash, J.	Bull, W.	Crewe, H.
Asleworth, W.	Bunney, F.	Crick, E.
Atherton, A. J. B.	Burdock, E. C.	Cripps, H.
Atkinson, J.	Burgess, W.	Cross, W.
Atkinson, J. H.	Burnett, H. N.	Crowther, J. E.
Austin, L.	Burns, E.	Crumpling, J.
Baldwin, A. H., M.M.	Burton, W. H.	Cudworth, R.
Ball, W.	Butcher, A.	Culm, F.
Banfield, F. W.	Butler, G. F.	Daley, P.
Banister, F. C.	Butler, J. T.	Daniels, R.
Barker, P. J.	Byrne, H.	Darby, F.
Barley, A. C.	Byrne, T.	Davies, G. M.
Barnes, R. E. V.	Cameron, T.	Davies, J. R.
Bass, G. F.	Capstick, E.	Dawson, G. E.
Baxter, N.	Carr. R.	Deeming, A.
Beaumont, G. L.	Carrington, C. F.	Derrick, A. D.
Bell, N. T.	Cartwright, G.	Devine, G.
Benjamin, I.	Caudle, C. V.	Devonport, G. F.
Benning, W. A.	Chapell, H.	Dey, J.
Bentham, F.	Chapman, R. T.	Dinsdale, H.
Berstone, A. E.	Chapman, W. W.	Dixon, G.
Berry, A. E.	Charman, S.	Dixon, J. W.
Beswick, R.	Child, J. J.	Dodd, C. T.
Blackband, H.	Clarke, L.	Dodd, S.
Bloomfield, J.	Clayton, W.	Dorey, H.
Bonner, E. J.	Clear, A.	Doughty, H.
Boot, A.	Clemence, H.	Douglas, T. H.

NOMINAL ROLL—continued.

NAME.

Dove, W.
Doyle, A. J.
Duckett, C. B.
Duggan, H.
Eccles, J. T.
Eddlestone, W.
Edgar, A.
Edward, J.
Edwards, F.
Elliott, A. H.
Elwell, J. T.
Entwistle, E.
Etherington, H.
Everett, G.
Fagg, F. S.
Fairhurst, J.
Fairminer, A.
Falconbridge, A.
Falk, W. J.
Falkingham, C.
Farquharson, G.
Fenton, A. C.
Fern, J.
Fielder, R. C.
Fifield, A. S.
Flippance, W.
Foote, R. J.
Foster, E.
Foster, F. C.
Foster, J.
Francis, W. J.
Franks, C.
Freeman, J.
Gage, F. W.
Gallop, J. T.
Galloway, A.
Gant, A.
Gardner, A. H.
Gardner, R.
Gellatly, F.
Gem, G. F.
Giles, S.
Gillett, A.
Godley, A.
Goodridge, H.
Goodwin, F.

NAME.

Gordon, J.
Gray, F.
Gray, J.
Grayling, J. A.
Greatorex, E.
Green, R. B.
Greenfield, J. E.
Gricewood, C.
Hadwyn, J.
Hall, A.
Hall, A. G.
Hansell, H.
Harding, J.
Harding, T.
Harman, H. J.
Harris, W. (293269)
Harris, W. (2082)
Harrison, J. T.
Hartland, W. A.
Hartshorne, J.
Hassell, E.
Hawkins, T. W.
Hayes, A.
Hayes, W.
Haywood, H.
Hazel, G. W.
Heal, F. H.
Heath, W. H.
Hebblethwaite, H.
Helps, W. B.
Henderson, F.
Henderson, R.
Henderson, W.
Hepworth, A.
Heslop, H.
Higgins, R. C.
Hill, A.
Hill, P.
Hill, T. J.
Hinchliffe, G.
Hodgkinson, R.
Hodgson, T.
Hollingworth, H.
Holloway, W.
Hoole, J.
Hopkins, F. C.

NAME.

Hopkins, J. B.
Hotton, A.
Howard, T.
Howieson, W.
Hoy, W. A.
Hughes, A.
Hughes, H. J.
Hulme, F.
Ibbotson, H.
Iliffe, N. F.
Ilott, S.
Inglis, D. C., M.S.M.
Innes, J.
Irvine, W.
Jack, J. M.
Jackson, W.
Jarvis, A. E.
Johnson, G.
Jones, L. V. C.
Jones, W.
Jordan, E.
Jowers, E.
Juggins, E.
Keefe, T.
Keeley, R.
Kelly, E.
Kemp, J. W.
Kender, R.
Kerly, F. E.
Killen, A. W. G.
Kincherton, W. J.
Kingerly, G.
Kingdon, J. W.
Knott, W. H.
Lancaster, G., M.M.
Land, R. S.
Lane, H. P.
Langer, W. G.
Lannigan, J.
Lawson, W.
Lawton, W.
Lee, A. B.
Lewis, R.
Lewis, S.
Littley, C.
Llewellin, G. W.

NOMINAL ROLL—continued.

NAME.	NAME.	NAME.
Lockley, A., M.M.	Morgan, O.	Robert, N. D.
Lockyer, A.	Morland, A.	Robinson, G. S.
Lodge, T.	Morley, A.	Robson, W. D.
Loker, W. A.	Morton, W.	Rodgers, A. E.
Lupson, G. P.	Moss, W. E.	Ross, D.
Lynch, H.	Mullins, R.	Ross, T. F.
Lyon, G.	Napper, F.	Rumble, A. G.
Macken, G. C.	Natham, M.	Salberg, H.
Maddock, H. S.	Nattrass, F.	Scotson, J.
Maddocks, J.	Nicholson, A.	Scott, D.
Makin, J.	Niell, G. H.	Self, F. A.
Mann, G.	Nitebexon, J. A.	Sessions, J.
Manners, F. G.	O'Brien, P.	Sexton, J.
Manning, E. J. C.	O'Donald, R. A.	Sharp, P.
Mansell, J.	Overton, L. M.	Shaw, T.
Margetts, H. H.	Owen, W. J.	Sheehan, D.
Markham, P.	Pacey, L.	Shipman, W.
Marsh, A. G.	Parmenter, A. C.	Sims, T.
* Marshall, F.	Pashley, T.	Sippetts, A.
Marshall, T.	Payne, G. A.	Skinner, F. J.
Martin, A. L.	Pearson, W. E.	Slinger, H. M.
Martin, J. C.	Peck, C. S.	Smart, A.
Marples, T.	Penny, J. J.	Smith, B.
Masters, S.	Pickering, O.	Smith, G.
Mauchlin, G.	Pike, J. E.	Smith, J. A.
McBean, J.	Plank, G. H.	Smith, S.
McDonald, J.	Powlesland, W. A.	Smith, T.
McFarlane, G. B.	Price, F. J.	Smith, W. H.
McGowan, T.	Price, H. H.	Spooner, W. J.
MacKay, B. J.	Pryor, H.	Stevens, H.
McKay, L. N.	Purvis, W. T.	Stewart, J.
McKendrick, J.	Quinton, W.	Stokoe, L.
McKenzie, N. R.	Raine, P.	Stoner, W.
McKeon, J.	Ramsden, L.	Stone, A. S.
McMinn, J.	Randall, A.	Stubbs, R. H.
McRae,	Rankin, T.	Styles, E. H.
McVay, T.	Ravenhill, J.	Summers, A. H.
Medley, H.	Rawlinson, H.	Sutcliffe, H. W.
Merrill, W. A.	Rayen, W. H.	Swindley, F. H.
Midson, F. W.	Reed, F. C.	Swindley, J. H.
Mills, A. C.	Reid, R.	Tapping, W.
Mills, G. H.	Renneson, S. R.	Taylor, A.
Mills, W. G.	Reynolds, A. J.	Taylor, D.
Milner, P. C.	Richardson, C.	Taylor, H. B.
Mitcheson, J.	Riddle, R.	Taylor, M.
Modley, F.	Rimmer, J.	Taylor, O.

NOMINAL ROLL—continued.

NAME.	NAME.	NAME.
Taylor, W. H.	Wainwright, J.	Whitcombe, F. A.
Taylor, W. J.	Walker, H. G.	White, J.
Thomas, H. C.	Walker, J.	White, L.
Thomas, J.	Walker, P.	Whitehead, E.
Thompson, J.	Wallis, F. W.	Wickenden, C.
Thompson, W. J.	Walls, G.	Wilcox, H.
Tideswell, A.	Walter, T. W.	Wilcox, P. J.
Timms, W. H.	Ward, G.	Wild, E.
Todd, J.	Watts, J.	Wilks, A.
Tompkinson, A.	Waughman, H.	Williams, R.
Tongs, W. J.	Webb, F. J.	Williams, T.
Townsend, A. E.	Weekly, M. A.	Wilmot, J.
Townsend, M.	Weeks, S.	Wilson, H.
Trench, T. P.	Weight, L. H.	Wilson, J. (183312).
Tucker, S.	Weight, W. P.	Wilson, J. (206127).
Tully, P.	Wells, E.	Wiltshire, H.
Tull, G. H.	West, A.	Winter, W.
Turnbull, J.	West, J. F.	Wood, H.
Tuttlebury, W.	West, T. D.	Woodford, T. C.
Unsworth, J. E.	Westmorland, H.	Woolley, W.
Varcoe, A.	Wetherall, R.	Worrall, A. E.
Vernon, C. H.	Whayman, J.	Wragg, L.
Vernon, F.	Wheatley, E.	Wright, F. N.
Waghorn, W. (2459)	Whelan, T. J.	
Waghorn, W. (277429)	Whitcombe, A.	

478

Wyman & Sons Ltd., Printers, London, Reading and Fakenham.

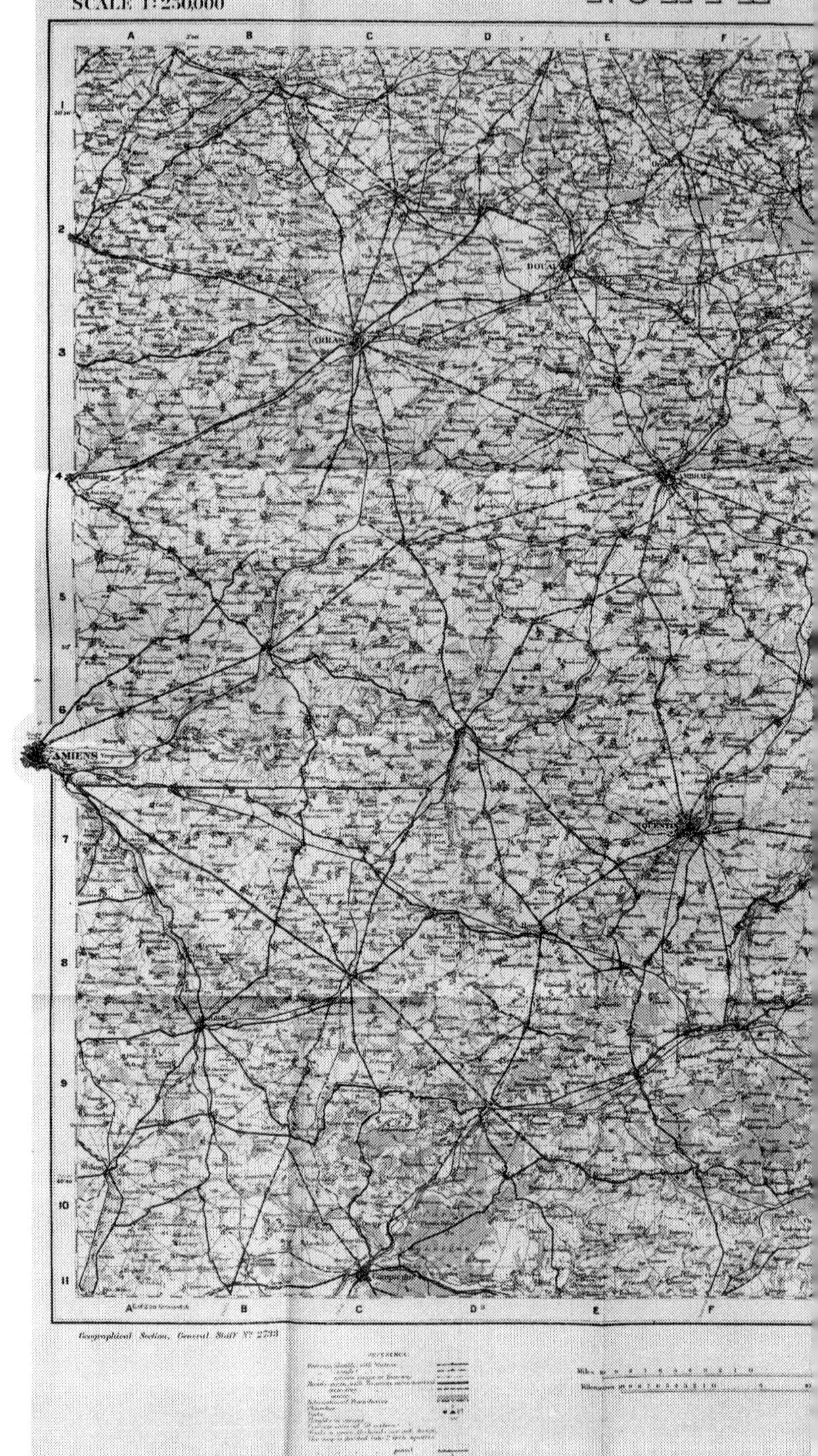
SCALE 1:250,000
NORTH
A
B
C
D
E
F
1
2
3
4
5
6
7
8
9
10
11
DOUAI
AMIENS
Geographical Section, General Staff No 2733

EUROPE

SHEET 4.

www.ingramcontent.com/pod-product-compliance
Lightning Source LLC
Chambersburg PA
CBHW060422100426
42812CB00030B/3273/J

* 9 7 8 1 8 4 7 3 4 4 9 0 8 *